The Manufacturing Guides
Product and Furniture Design

Rob Thompson

With the participation of Young-Yun Kim

The Manufacturing Guides

Product and Furniture Design

Contents

Page 2, clockwise from top left: Laser cutting the Luceplan Queen Titania light; vacuum metalizing colours; ultrasonic welding the A cover and window of the TSM 6 mobile phone; and assembling Rega speaker cabinets.

First published in the United Kingdom in 2011 by Thames & Hudson Ltd, 181A High Holborn, London WC1V 7QX

British Library Cataloguing-in-Publication Data
A catalogue record for this book is available from the British Library

ISBN 978-0-500-28919-8

Printed and bound in China by Toppan Leefung Printing Limited

To find out about all our publications, please visit **www.thamesandhudson.com**. There you can subscribe to our e-newsletter, browse or download our current catalogue, and buy any titles that are in print.

Part One
Forming Technology

How to use this book

This guidebook is intended as a source of inspiration in the process of design for manufacture. Established and new mass-production techniques are covered. The case studies demonstrate the scope for creativity within the confines of mechanized manufacturing and the process illustrations highlight some of the technical considerations.

How to use the processes sections

Each process is introduced and a brief outline of the key reasons why it may have been selected are put forward. The description focuses on the conventional application of each technology. It is up to the designer to challenge established ways of working where feasible.

The book is divided into three parts (colour coded for ease of reference): forming technology (blue), joining technology (orange) and finishing technology (yellow).

The technical illustration shows the inner working of the technology. These principles are fundamental and define the technical constraints of the tools and equipment. Each technique within a process, such as gas-assisted injection molding (page 42) and multishot injection molding (page 44), are individually explored and technically explained.

(page 42)
(page 44)

Essential Information

VISUAL QUALITY	●●●●●○○
SPEED	●●●○○○○
TOOLING COST	●●●○○○○
UNIT COST	●●●○○○
ENVIRONMENT	●●●●○○○

Related processes include:
• Cut Foam

Alternative and competing processes include:
• CNC Machining
• Expanded Polystyrene (EPS) Molding
• Injection Molding
• Reaction Injection Molding

Essential Information
A rough guide to five key features of each process to help inform designers and aid decision-making.

How to use the essential information panels

In addition, the opening pages include a detailed essential information panel. This defines comparable values for the five key features of each process, which are visual quality, speed, tooling cost, unit cost and environmental impacts. The scoring system is relative and based on one point being the lowest and seven points being the highest. Of course, the type of product, application and context of use will affect these values. They are intended as a rough guide to help inform designers and aid decision-making.

The individual techniques are listed and in many cases explored in more detail on subsequent pages. Similar processes are often referred to by different names. Where possible, these have been explained and the most fitting process title has been used. For example, investment casting (page 66) is used to describe the high-volume production of metal casting in expendable ceramic molds, whereas lost wax casting is used by jewellers, sculptors and artists to describe the same technique when it is used to manufacture prototypes, low volumes and works of art.

How to use the case studies

The real-life case studies feature factories from around the world. They demonstrate some of the most innovative technologies currently being used. Each of these processes is utilized in the production of well-known products, furniture and lighting designs. The processes are covered by a step-by-step description and analysis of the key stages. The principal attributes of each technology are described in detail and some of the extended qualities, such as scale and material scope, are outlined where necessary.

Photographs of geometry, detail, colour and surface finish are used to show the many ways that each

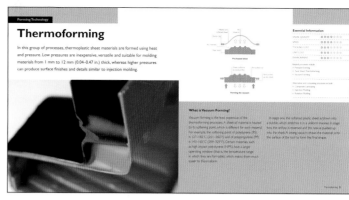

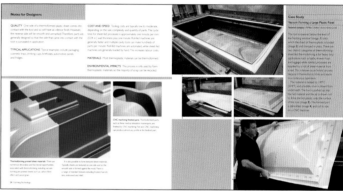

Processes and Case Studies Each manufacturing technology is described in detail with a technical illustration and a case study by a leading manufacturer. This example demonstrates the scope and opportunities of thermoforming, including vacuum forming, pressure forming and twin sheet thermoforming.

process can be applied. Leading products demonstrate what the finished article looks like to the consumer.

Relevant links between the processes, such as forming and finishing operations, are highlighted in the text. It is essential that designers are aware of the wide range of manufacturing opportunities at their disposal. This information provides a well-informed starting point for further focused investigation, which is essential if designers are to harness the full potential each manufacturing technology.

Introduction

This book equips designers with knowledge about some of the most exciting manufacturing processes and material technologies utilized in the production of everyday objects.

Factories are a source of inspiration. The processes explored in this book include mass-production techniques such as die casting (page 62), injection molding (page 38), plastic extrusion (page 34) and ceramic press molding (page 100), where the tooling costs are too high for prototyping and low-volume applications. It also includes processes that may not have high tooling costs, but have been optimized for mass production.

Every manufactured item must strike a balance between materials and processes. The role of designers is to tailor product development, from conception to production, to meet this challenge with innovative solutions.

Knowledge about materials and manufacturing

The technologies presented in this book are a valuable source of knowledge for any designer. A fundamental step in the design process is translating concepts into objects that can be shaped and assembled by mass-production processes. Knowledge about materials and manufacturing technology will ensure that the design vision is maintained and not compromised when

Pedalite exploded This bicycle pedal light, named Pedalite, is powered by an energy storage capacitor and microgenerator rather than a chemical battery. It was designed by Product Partners in conjunction with the toolmaker and molder (ENL Limited). A close working partnership between these two ensured the design vision was successfully translated through the design, development and toolmaking process.

confronted with the realities of mass production. In addition, knowledge about materials and processes enables designers to challenge the mechanics and manufacturing with intelligent and innovative solutions that may otherwise have gone unexplored.

Every mass-produced article has undergone a process of realization, development and refinement. This can be decoded and understood by designers who have an awareness of how things are made. This insight is invaluable for inspiring new projects, highlighting where improvements can be made and any errors that need to be avoided.

There is a rich choice of materials and processes and almost anything can be manufactured with endless finance. Reality is that there are very tight budgets and mass-produced products must be designed to utilize materials efficiently and cost effectively. The cost implications of inefficient design and engineering for high volumes, such as 40 million units, would be catastrophic: $0.01 inefficiency leads to $400,000 in this case. Similarly, every ounce of additional material requires more natural resources and energy to be consumed and produces more waste materials.

Designers alone cannot undertake this challenge. It is essential that all the necessary skills be employed from the start. Therefore, designers need to speak the 'language' of engineers, mechanics, molders, fabricators, materials suppliers and anyone else that might be involved. This book is a step in that learning process.

Bang & Olufsen speakers The vivid colours of these Bang & Olufsen BeoLab 4000 speakers are produced by anodizing aluminium. Anodizing can be applied to all types of finishes and textures, including satin, brushed, embossed and mirror polished.

Mass-production techniques

Injection molding remains the most widely used forming process for commodity plastics. It is utilized in the manufacture of a huge variety of different products, whose shape and size can range from tiny medical devises to lorry bumpers.

There are many variants of injection molding that widen the scope of possibilities for designers, including gas-assisted (page 42), multishot (page 44) and in-mold decoration (page 46).

Metal injection molding (page 48) combines the processing advantages of injection molding with the physical characteristics of metals. It is thereby possible to form complex shapes, with intricate surface details and precise dimensions.

The surface of metals can be chemically changed, added to or subtracted from with dramatic effect. For example, anodizing (page 170) is an electrochemical process used to oxidize the surface of aluminium. Once formed, the layer of aluminium oxide ceramic can be dyed with a range of bright colours (see above).

HTC Legend The aluminium body on the HTC Legend is sculpted from a partially formed block of aluminium by CNC machining. This results in a seamless finish with precise dimensions.

Wood is a highly desirable material, but it grows naturally and so each piece will bend, cut and finish slightly differently. Steam bending (page 108) is a mass-production technique that is sympathetic to these qualities and utilizes the strength and lightness of wood. The grain runs continuously along the entire length of a bentwood part. By contrast, a sawn timber profile (CNC machining, page 112) will have had its lengths of grain cut through, thus shortening them and weakening the structure as a whole.

Bentwood production was industrialized by Michael Thonet in the 1850s, with the production of chair type No. 14 (see below).

Thonet 214 Chair type No. 14 (now known as 214) was designed by Michael Thonet in 1859. He was a pioneer of mass production; more than 50 million No. 14 chairs were sold within the first 50 years of production. It is one of the most successful mass-produced chairs in the world to date.

Computer-aided manufacture (CAM)

Most modern manufacturing techniques are computer-guided. Computer-aided manufacturing (CAM) has contributed towards developments in speed, efficiency and repeatability. CAM has also made it possible to manufacture large volumes of products that would have previously only been possible in small quantities. For example, CNC machining (page 112) is precise and versatile and can be utilized to shape a range of materials. The importance of this technology, for high-volume applications, has increased in recent years as it has become more sophisticated and efficient. As a result of considered design and by combining multiple parts and operations into a single process it has been possible to utilize this technology to manufacture consumer products in large volumes, such as the innovative HTC Legend mobile phone (see above).

Computer-aided design (CAD)

Computer software plays an important role in the design and engineering of parts for mass production. Predicting and testing the quality of the finished part has become more reliable with developments in simulation software based on finite element analysis (FEA).

The forming of many products is simulated using FEA to maximize the efficiency of the operation. FEA software is not used in all forming applications, but it does have many advantages. Most importantly, it reduces tooling costs because parts can be molded 'right first time' (see below).

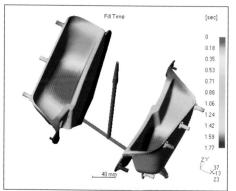

Moldflow analysis
The colour scale on the automotive interior product manufactured by Resinex and Gärtner & Lang indicates fill time in seconds. Appearance is very important, so the flow analysis software was used to eliminate weld lines and colour variation in critical areas.

Design realization

In the process of design for mass production parts will be prototyped and may be manufactured in low volumes to begin with; 3D realization is a fundamental step in the creative product development process.

Parts designed for mass production that require very expensive tooling, such as for injection molding and die casting, can, for example, be prototyped by vacuum casting and rapid prototyping. These technologies have relatively low tooling costs, but the unit costs are many times higher and the mechanical and visual qualities may be different.

Decisions about what processes and materials to use in the realization of a product are governed by projected volumes, geometry, size, performance requirements and aesthetic qualities. This book features case studies from leading manufacturers from around the world. Every original object challenges their technical experts in new and exciting ways. It is up to designers to ensure that these challenges promote innovative solutions for the good of everyone.

Forming Technology

Compression Molding

In this process rubber, plastic and fibre-reinforced composite are shaped by squeezing them into a pre-heated die cavity. Compression molding is generally used for thermosetting materials.

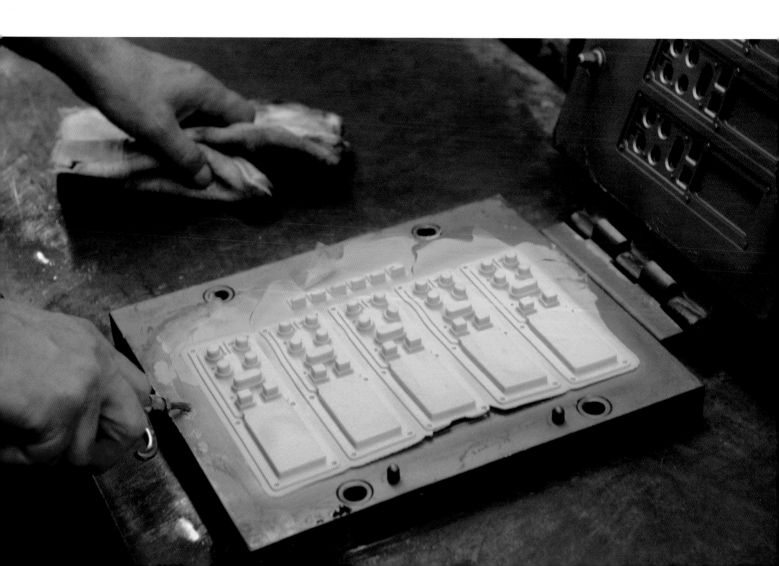

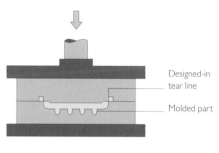

Moving platen

Measure of
conditioned
rubber

Static platen

Designed-in
tear line

Molded part

Stage 1: Load

Stage 2: Mold

Essential Information

VISUAL QUALITY	●●●●●●○○○
SPEED	●●●●●○○○○
TOOLING COST	●●●●●○○○○
UNIT COST	●●●●○○○○○
ENVIRONMENT	●●●●●○○○○

Related processes include:

• Dough Molding Compound (DMC)
• Plastic Compression Molding
• Rubber Compression Molding
• Sheet Molding Compound (SMC)

Alternative and competing processes include:

• Composite Laminating
• Filament Winding
• Injection Molding
• Reaction Injection Molding

What is Rubber Compression Molding?

In stage one, the rubber is conditioned to remove any crystallinity that might have built up since its production. Then a measure of conditioned rubber is placed in the lower mold. In stage two, the two halves of the mold are brought together and pressure is applied gradually to encourage the material to flow. After ten minutes the rubber is fully cured and its molecular structure is formed.

Tear lines are integrated into the design to reduce secondary operations. They ensure that the flash separates in a consistent manner when it is removed and so leaves a tidy edge detail.

QUALITY This is a high-quality process. Many of the characteristics can be attributed to the materials, such as heat-resistant and electrically insulating phenolics, flexible and resilient silicones or high-strength fibre-reinforced polyesters.

TYPICAL APPLICATIONS The spectrum of compatible materials results in a range of applications, such as keypads, seals, electrical housing, kitchen equipment and light fittings. Combined with compression molding, DMC and SMC have been used to replace steel and aluminium in applications such as automotive bodywork and structural electronic enclosures.

COST AND SPEED Tooling costs are expensive, but much less expensive than for injection molding. For plastics, cycle time is very rapid and usually about two minutes per part. By contrast, rubbers take considerably longer and often need to be left in the heated press for ten minutes or more.

MATERIALS Thermosetting materials including phenolic, polyester, epoxy, urea, melamine and rubber. The molding process for themoplastics is slightly different because they have to be plasticized and formed.

ENVIRONMENTAL IMPACTS Thermosetting plastics require high molding temperatures, typically around 180°C (356°F). It is not possible to recycle thermosets directly, due to their molecular structure.

Integrating colour details An advantage of compression molding rubber is that it is possible to integrate a range of colours. They are either introduced as a pre-form, such as buttons or logos, or are molded in the same sequence, in which case the weld line is irregular (as shown here) and tends to be covered in the final application.

1

2

3

Case Study

Compression Molding Silicone Keypads

Featured company RubberTech2000
www.rubbertech2000.co.uk

Silicone rubber is extruded, conditioned and pre-formed into pellets. The pellets are inserted into each mold cavity (image **1**).

The two halves of the tool are brought together and placed under a press (image **2**). The tool takes about ten minutes to reach 180°C (356°F). Cross-linking takes place as a result of time and pressure. The mold is removed from the press and opened (image **3**). Once they have been demolded, the parts are packed for shipping (image **4**). They will be 'torn' from the flash when they are finally assembled.

4

What is Plastic Compression Molding?

In stage one, a pre-formed pellet is loaded into the die cavity. Phenolic powder is prepared by compressing it into pellets, which are heated up to around 100°C (212°F) in preparation for molding.

In stage two, the upper tool is gradually forced into the die cavity in a steady process. The material plasticizes at approximately 115°C (239°F) and is cured when it reaches 150°C (302°F).

Compression molding plastic is a simple operation and yet it is suitable for the production of complex parts. It operates at high pressure, ranging from 40 to 400 tonnes (40–441 US tons).

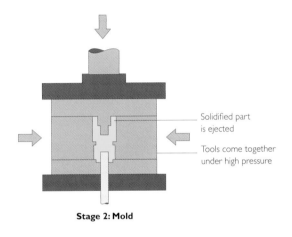

Hydraulic ram

Moving platen

Measure of powder or pre-formed pellet

Side action tool

Static platen

Stage 1: Load

Solidified part is ejected

Tools come together under high pressure

Stage 2: Mold

Colourful recycled plastics These colourful Smile Plastics sheet materials are manufactured by compression molding. They are made up of thermoplastic materials which require a slightly different molding process because they are plasticized and formed. Chips of recycled industrial and post-consumer waste are placed into a mold, heated and compressed. The different-coloured materials do not mix completely during heating and compression. Many thermoplastics can be pre-processed in this way.

1

Compression Molding an Outdoor Lamp Housing

Featured company Cromwell Plastics
www.cromwell-plastics.co.uk

The lower half of the compression tool is made up of three parts: one static and two side action (image **1**). The three parts are brought together to form the die cavity into which the phenolic pellets are placed (images **2** and **3**). The upper mold is forced into the die cavity and after two minutes the mold separates to reveal the formed and fully cured resin.

The final lamp housings, which include brass electrical contacts that are inserted post-molding, demonstrate the high level of finish that can be achieved with this process (image **4**).

2

3

4

What is DMC and SMC Compression Molding?

The diagram illustrates DMC compression molding. SMC is a similar process, except that it is used for sheet profiles as opposed to bulk shapes. The molding compound is a mixture of fibre reinforcement and thermosetting resin: DMC is made up of chopped fibre reinforcement, whereas SMC contains sheets of woven fibre reinforcement.

The sequence of operation is the same for both. In stage one, a measure of DMC or SMC is loaded into the die cavity in the lower tool. Metal inserts with locating pins are loaded into slots.

In stage two, the upper tool is gradually forced into the die cavity. Thermosetting material plasticizes at approximately 115°C (239°F) and is cured when it reaches 150°C (302°F), which takes two to five minutes. In stage three, the parts of the mold separate in sequence. If necessary, the part is relieved from the lower or upper tool with ejector pins.

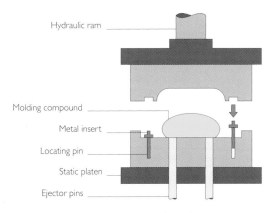

Hydraulic ram

Molding compound

Metal insert

Locating pin

Static platen

Ejector pins

Stage 1: Load

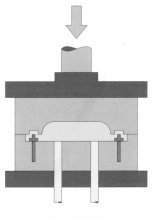

Stage 2: Mold

Varying wall thickness Step changes in wall thickness are not a problem with DMC molding. Wall thickness can range from 1 mm to 50 mm (0.04–1.97 in.). It is limited by the exothermic nature of the thermosetting reaction because thick wall sections are prone to blistering and other defects as a direct result of the catalytic reaction. It is generally better to reduce wall thickness and minimize material consumption, therefore bulky parts are hollowed out or inserts are added. However, some applications require thick wall sections such as parts that have to withstand high levels of dielectric vibration.

1

2

DMC Compression Molding 8-pin Rings

Featured company Cromwell Plastics
www.cromwell-plastics.co.uk

This is a DMC compression molding operation. The DMC is polyester and fibreglass based (image **1**). A predetermined measure is loaded into the die (image **2**).

The two halves of the die come together to force the DMC to fill the die cavity. After curing, the molds separate to reveal the fully formed part (image **3**). Removing the cured part reveals brass inserts which have been over-molded (image **4**). The locating pins, which protrude from the surface of the part, are unscrewed.

The final parts are deflashed (image **5**).

3

4

5

Thermoforming

In this group of processes, thermoplastic sheet materials are formed using heat and pressure. Low pressures are inexpensive, versatile and suitable for molding materials from 1 mm to 12 mm (0.04–0.47 in.) thick, whereas higher pressures can produce surface finishes and details similar to injection molding.

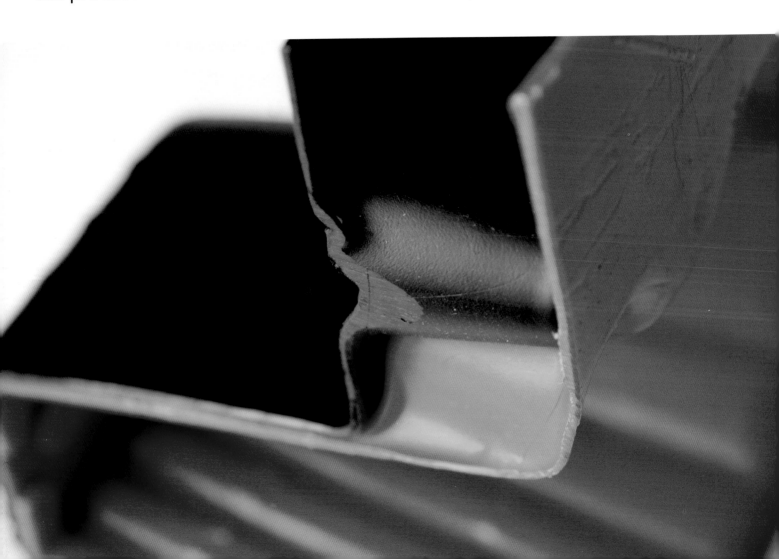

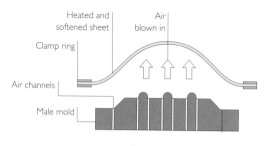

Heated and
softened sheet

Air
blown in

Clamp ring

Air channels

Male mold

Pre-heated sheet

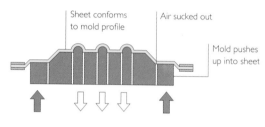

Sheet conforms
to mold profile

Air sucked out

Mold pushes
up into sheet

Forming the vacuum

Essential Information

VISUAL QUALITY	●●●●●●●○
SPEED	●●●●●○○
TOOLING COST	●●●●●○○
UNIT COST	●●●●○○○
ENVIRONMENT	●●●○○○○

Related processes include:
- Pressure Forming
- Twin Sheet Thermoforming
- Vacuum Forming

Alternative and competing processes include:
- Composite Laminating
- Injection Molding
- Rotation Molding

What is Vacuum Forming?

Vacuum forming is the least expensive of the thermoforming processes. A sheet of material is heated to its softening point, which is different for each material. For example, the softening point of polystyrene (PS) is 127–182°C (261–360°F) and of polypropylene (PP) is 143–165°C (289–329°F). Certain materials, such as high impact polystyrene (HIPS), have a larger operating window (that is, the temperature range in which they are formable), which makes them much easier to thermoform.

In stage one, the softened plastic sheet is blown into a bubble, which stretches it in a uniform manner. In stage two, the airflow is reversed and the tool is pushed up into the sheet. A strong vacuum draws the material onto the surface of the tool to form the final shape.

Notes for Designers

QUALITY One side of a thermoformed plastic sheet comes into contact with the tool and so will have an inferior finish. However, the reverse side will be smooth and unmarked. Therefore, parts are generally designed so that the side that came into contact with the tool is concealed in application.

TYPICAL APPLICATIONS Typical examples include packaging, cosmetic trays, drinking cups, briefcases, automotive panels and fridges.

COST AND SPEED Tooling costs are typically low to moderate, depending on the size, complexity and quantity of parts. The cycle time for sheet-fed processes is approximately one minute per mm (0.04 in.) wall thickness plus one minute. Roll-fed machines are generally faster and multiple cavity tools can make hundreds of parts per minute. Roll-fed machines are automated, while sheet-fed machines are generally loaded by hand. This increases labour costs.

MATERIALS Most thermoplastic materials can be thermoformed.

ENVIRONMENTAL IMPACTS This process is only used to form thermoplastic materials, so the majority of scrap can be recycled.

CNC machining finished parts Thermoformed parts, such as these medical simulation mannequins, are finished by CNC machining. Five-axis CNC machining can produce almost any profile in the finished part.

Thermoforming printed sheet materials There are numerous decorative and functional opportunities associated with thermoforming, including vacuum forming pre-printed sheets such as carbon fibre-effect and wood grain.

It is also possible to form textured sheet materials. Typically sheets are textured on one side and so the smooth side is formed against the mold. There is a range of standard textures including frosted, haircell, lens, embossed and relief.

1

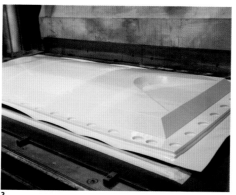

2

3

Case Study

Vacuum Forming a Large Plastic Panel

Featured company MiMtec Limited www.mimtec.co.uk

The tool is lowered below the level of the 'molding window' (image **1**) onto which the sheet of thermoplastic is loaded (image **2**) and clamped in place. There are two distinct categories of thermoforming: sheet-fed thermoforming is for heavy duty applications such as baths, shower trays and luggage; while roll-fed processes are supplied by a roll of sheet material from a reel. This is known as an 'in-line' process because it thermoforms, trims and stacks in a continuous operation.

The material is heated to 190°C (374°F) and a bubble of air is blown from underneath. The tool is pushed up into the hot material and the air is drawn out to force the hot plastic onto the surface of the tool (image **3**). The formed part is demolded (image **4**) and cut to size on a CNC machine.

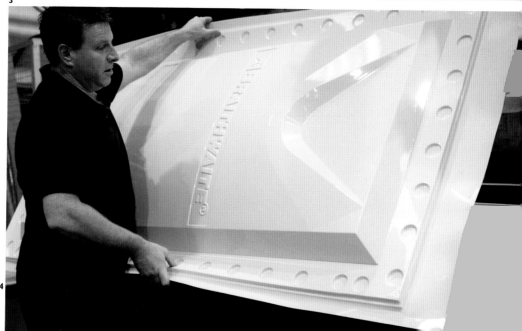

4

What is Pressure Forming?

Pressure forming is the reverse of vacuum forming: the sheet is formed onto the surface of the mold under up to six bar (87 psi) of air pressure. This means that a greater level of detail can be achieved. Surface details on the mold will be reproduced with much more accuracy than vacuum forming. Surface finish can be more accurately controlled and is therefore functional.

However, like vacuum forming, only one side of the sheet will be functional.

Higher pressure means that more complex and intricate details can be molded, including surface textures. This process is capable of producing parts similar to injection molding at lower volumes.

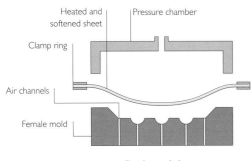

Pre-heated sheet

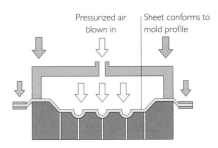

Forming the vacuum

Case Study

Pressure Forming a Door Panel

Featured company MiMtec Limited
www.mimtec.co.uk

The door panel is molded in 5 mm (0.2 in.) thick acrylonitrile butadiene styrene (ABS) (image **1**). Pressure forming is required to form the undercut created by incorporating a handle. To form the undercut an insert is used in the mold so the part can be demolded with minimal stress. It is re-assembled after each molding cycle (image **2**).

The sheet of ABS is loaded onto the tool (image **3**) and clamped in place. The heaters are individually controlled (image **4**) to ensure that each part of the sheet stretches exactly the right amount during forming. The sheet is heated to 140°C (284°F) and once up to temperature a vacuum is drawn from underneath and pressure is applied from above. The finished part is removed from the mold (image **5**) and is ready to be trimmed.

Pressure forming undercuts in a screen surround (left)
Pressure forming is used to mold parts with undercuts and other features not feasible with vacuum forming. A split mold is required to mold this screen surround so that it can be demolded in one piece.

Intricate and well-defined surface details (right)
Higher pressure means that more complex and intricate details can be molded, including EDM (electrical discharge machined) or 'spark eroded' surface textures, sharp corners and logos.

2

3

4

5

What is Twin Sheet Thermoforming?

In twin sheet thermoforming two sheets are thermoformed and clamped together. This forms an enclosed and thin-walled product. Both sides of the product are functional, unlike the single-sheet processes.

The machines are rotary. The clamps transfer the sheet into the heating chamber, where it is raised to softening temperature; it is then thermoformed and clamped and finally rotated to the unloading station. The two sheets are thermoformed individually, one above the other. Once fully formed, they are clamped together. Residual heat from the thermoforming enables the bond to form with prolonged contact. The bond has similar strength to the parent material.

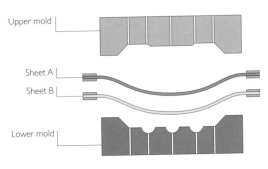

Upper mold | Sheet A | Sheet B | Lower mold

Pre-heated sheets

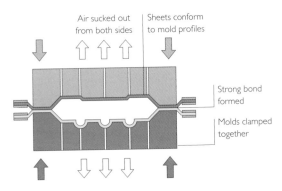

Air sucked out from both sides | Sheets conform to mold profiles | Strong bond formed | Molds clamped together

Forming the vacuum and clamping

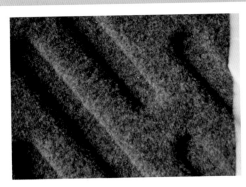

Carpet-covered thermoforming Carpet-covered thermoforming produced in a single operation by Kaysersberg Plastics.

Foam-filled Terracover® The Terracover® ice pallet is engineered to accommodate five tonnes of load over an area of only 150 × 150 mm (5.91 × 5.91 in.). It is used to cover ice rinks temporarily for concerts and events. Filling the cavity with foam further increases rigidity, strength and thermal insulation.

1

Featured company Kaysersberg Plastics
www.kaysersberg-plastics.com

Twin sheet thermoforming is the process of forming two sheets simultaneously and bonding them together to form hollow profiles. Two sheets of 4 mm (0.16 in.) thick high-density polyethylene (HDPE) are loaded and clamped separately (image **1**).

Sheet A is heated to softening point – 160°C (320°F) – and suspended below the upper thermoforming tool (image **2**), which is then vacuum formed (image **3**). Meanwhile, sheet B is vacuum formed over the lower tool. Just as they are both formed the molds come together and the residual heat bonds the two materials together (image **4**).

After four minutes the tools separate (image **5**). A small section demonstrates how sheets A and B (image **6**) are welded together across the surface with a series of spikes.

2

3

4

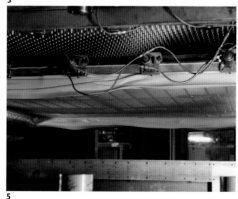

5

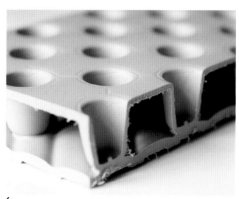

6

Rotation Molding

Rotation molding produces hollow forms with a constant wall thickness. Polymer powder is tumbled around inside the mold to produce virtually stress-free parts. Recent developments include in-mold graphics, lightweight foam walls and multi-layered wall sections.

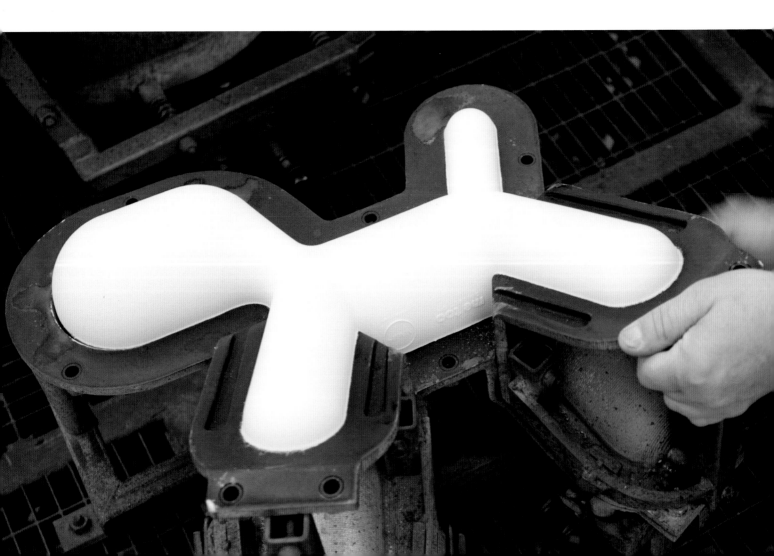

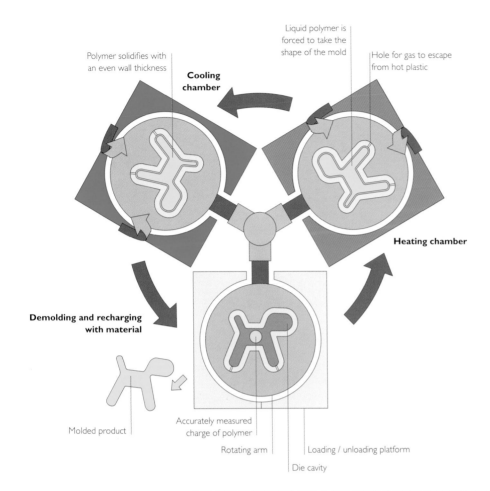

Polymer solidifies with an even wall thickness

Cooling chamber

Liquid polymer is forced to take the shape of the mold

Hole for gas to escape from hot plastic

Heating chamber

Demolding and recharging with material

Molded product

Accurately measured charge of polymer

Rotating arm

Die cavity

Loading / unloading platform

Essential Information

VISUAL QUALITY	●●●●●○○○
SPEED	●●●○○○○○
TOOLING COST	●●●●●●○○
UNIT COST	●●●●○○○○
ENVIRONMENT	●●●●○○○○

Alternative and competing processes include:

• Blow Molding
• Dip Molding
• Thermoforming

What is Rotation Molding?

A predetermined measure of polymer powder is dispensed evenly into each mold. It is closed, clamped and rotated into the heating chamber where it is heated up to around 250°C (482°F) for 25 minutes and is constantly rotated around its horizontal and vertical axes.

As the walls of the mold heat up the powder melts and gradually builds up an even coating on the inside surface. The rotating arm passes the molds onto the cooling chamber, where fresh air and moisture are pumped in to cool them for 25 minutes.

Once the parts have cooled sufficiently they are removed from the molds. The whole process takes between 30 and 90 minutes, depending on wall thickness and choice of material.

QUALITY Surface finish is good even though no pressure is applied. The molded product is almost stress free and has an even wall thickness. The plastic will shrink by 3% during the process, which may cause warpage in parts with large flat areas.

TYPICAL APPLICATIONS A variety of products including furniture, containers, bollards, planters and toys.

COST AND SPEED Tooling costs are relatively inexpensive: steel molds are the most expensive, followed by aluminium. Resin tools are the least expensive and suitable for production runs up to about 100 parts. Cycle time is usually between 30 and 90 minutes, depending on wall thickness and choice of material. Rotation molding is labour intensive. Fully automated molding is available for small parts and high volumes to reduce the costs.

MATERIALS Polyethylene (PE) is the most commonly rotation molded material. Many other thermoplastics can be used, such as polyamide (PA), polypropylene (PP) and polyvinyl chloride (PVC).

ENVIRONMENTAL IMPACTS Precise measures of powder are used to minimize scrap. Any thermoplastic scrap can be recycled. The tools stay clamped shut throughout the molding cycle. Even so, high temperatures are required to mold the polymer.

In-mold graphics for rotation molding In-mold graphics are applied to the surface of the mold prior to the raw material being loaded.

  The backing film bonds to the polymer during the molding process to create a seamless finish on the final product. This can eliminate secondary printing.

1

2

3

Rotation Molding the Magis Grande Puppy

Featured company Magis www.magisdesign.com

The Grande Puppy is being molded in green polyethylene (PE). A generous 3.6 kg (7.94 lb) of powder is used to ensure a wall thickness of 6 mm (0.236 in.), which makes it safe as a seat and children's toy. The mold is charged with the predetermined measure of powder (image **1**) and clamped shut. The molding sequence takes place: heating followed by cooling (image **2**). After cooling, the molds are separated (image **3**). The puppy is demolded and placed on a conveyor belt (image **4**) on its way to being deflashed and packaged.

4

Plastic Extrusion

Continuous lengths are extruded in a single material, or multiple materials, by co-extrusion. These processes are used to manufacture large volumes of products, including window frames, drain pipes, gaskets, tape, sheet and film. A wide range of thermoplastics and elastomers can be formed by extrusion.

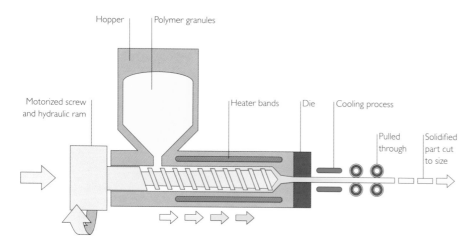

Hopper | Polymer granules

Motorized screw
and hydraulic ram

Heater bands | Die | Cooling process

Pulled
through

Solidified
part cut
to size

Essential Information

VISUAL QUALITY   ●●●●●○○○

SPEED   ●●●●●●○

TOOLING COST   ●●●●○○○○

UNIT COST   ●●●○○○○○

ENVIRONMENT   ●●●●○○○○

Related processes include:
• Blown Film Extrusion
• Co-extrusion
• Extrusion

Alternative and competing processes include:
• Filament Winding
• Injection Molding

What is Plastic Extrusion?

Similar to injection molding (page 38), polymer granules are fed from the hopper into the barrel, where they are simultaneously heated, mixed and moved towards the die by the rotating action of the Archimedean screw.

The melted plastic is forced through the profiled die at high pressure and through a sealed water tank, which cools and solidifies the polymer into the desired shape. It is drawn through the process by caterpillar tracks or threaded wheels.

Film and sheet extrusions are cooled as they pass through sets of cooling rolls, rather than a water tank. This helps to control the wall thickness and apply texture.

The extruded profile is cut to size or rolled up, depending on the flexibility of the material and application.

Notes for Designers

QUALITY The surface finish is semi-gloss and depends on the substrate and cooling process. Co-extruded materials are bonded together in the extrusion die and so form a strong hermetic bond.

It is possible to co-extrude up to five separate layers. This technique is used to combine the properties of the materials, such as improved resistance to ultraviolet (UV), soft touch or to provide a watertight seal.

TYPICAL APPLICATIONS The length of extrusion is virtually unlimited. This property has been utilized in the construction industry for drain pipes and door frames, for example. Tube, film, tape, sheet and coated wire are also extruded.

COST AND SPEED Tooling costs are moderate and less than for injection molding. Cycle time is relatively quick because, once up and running, this is a continuous process. Labour costs are relatively low. However, manual operations increase the costs.

MATERIALS Most thermoplastic materials can be extruded.

ENVIRONMENTAL IMPACTS Thermoplastic scrap can be directly recycled in this process. A high percentage of recycled material can be used in many applications, but there are restrictions for medical and food products.

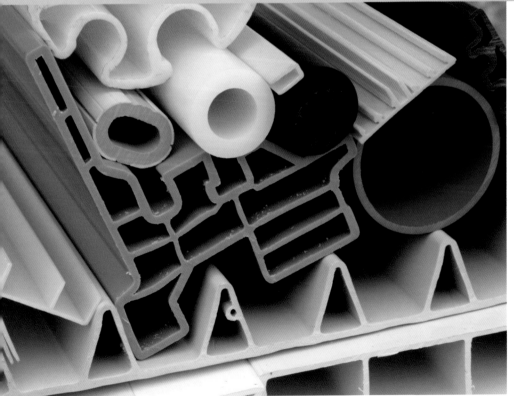

Extruded geometries Many types of geometry and different colours are possible with plastic extrusion as long as the wall section is reasonably constant and the profile is continuous. Large cross-sections are hollowed out using a pin or mandrel in the extrusion die. It is possible to co-extrude multiple materials and over-extrude onto rigid substrates such as metal wire.

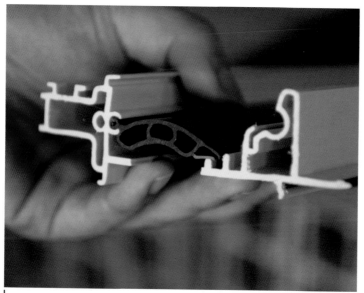

1

2

3

Case Study

Extruding a Window Frame

Featured company Ajin Tech www.apchul.com

This domestic window frame is extruded polyvinyl chloride (PVC) and is made in two main parts (image **1**).

The PVC granules (image **2**) are dried and fed into the hopper. As they pass through the barrel, forced along by the turning action of the Archimedean screw, they are precisely heated. The heating of each section of the barrel can be individually controlled (image **3**).

The die is made from tool steel, which can withstand the high temperatures. Typically, a die is made of two parts. This image depicts the upper half of the die (image **4**). Complex profiles with undercuts and hollow parts require more complex and expensive tooling.

The formed plastic is pushed through the die and simultaneously pulled to maintain an even wall thickness and to prevent the profile collapsing (image **5**).

4

5

Injection Molding

The leading process used for high-volume production of identical plastic products, injection molding is employed to produce a hugely diverse range of our day-to-day products. Complex shapes are achievable in a range of sizes, from large pieces of furniture to the tiniest widgets.

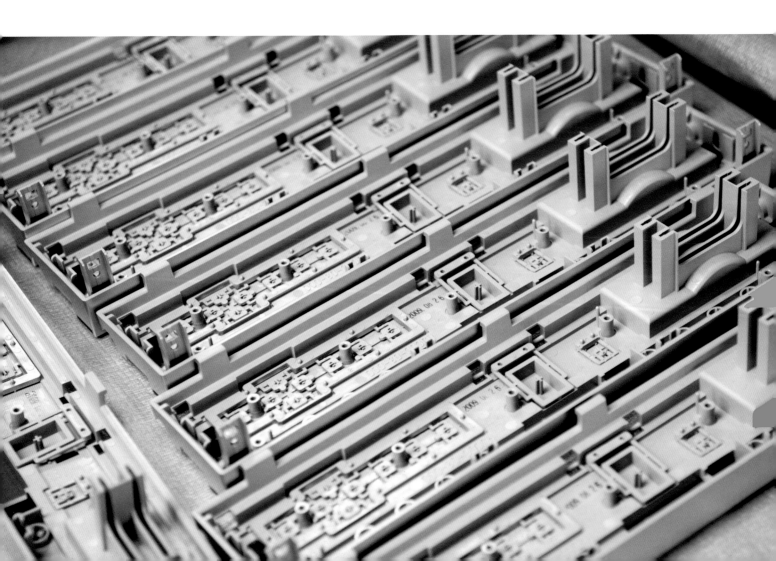

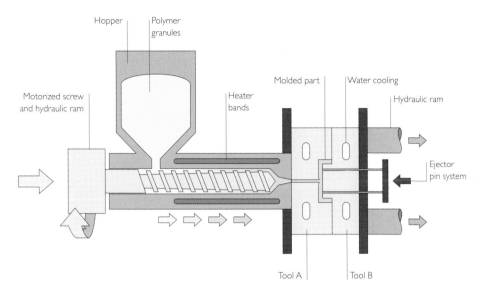

Hopper | Polymer granules

Motorized screw and hydraulic ram

Molded part | Water cooling

Heater bands

Hydraulic ram

Ejector pin system

Tool A | Tool B

Essential Information

QUALITY	⬤⬤⬤⬤⬤⬤⬤⬤◐⬤
SPEED	⬤⬤⬤⬤⬤⬤⬤⬤
TOOLING COST	⬤⬤⬤⬤⬤⬤⬤◐
UNIT COST	⬤⬤⬤◐⬤⬤◐⬤⬤
ENVIRONMENT	⬤⬤⬤⬤⬤◐◐⬤◐

Related processes include:

• Gas-assisted
• In-mold Decoration
• Multishot

Alternative and competing processes include:

• CNC Machining
• Compression Molding
• Foam Molding
• Plastic Extrusion
• Reaction Injection Molding
• Thermoforming
• Vacuum Casting

What is Injection Molding?

The polymer granules are fed from the hopper into the barrel where they are simultaneously heated, mixed and moved towards the mold by the rotating action of the Archimedean screw.

The melted plastic is injected through the gate and into the die cavity at high pressure.

To eject the part, the tools move apart, the cores retract and force is applied by the ejector pins to separate the part from the surface of the tool.

Tools and cores are generally machined from either aluminium or steel. Some cores are machined from copper, which has much better conductive qualities than aluminium or steel.

The least expensive injection molding tooling consists of two halves, known as the male tool and the female tool.

Notes for Designers

QUALITY The high pressure ensures good surface finish, fine reproduction of detail and, most importantly, excellent repeatability. The downside of the high pressure is that the resolidified polymer has a tendency to shrink and warp.

TYPICAL APPLICATIONS Injection molded parts can be found in every market sector, in particular, in automotive, industrial and household products. Products include shopping baskets, stationery, garden furniture, keypads and consumer electronic casings.

COST AND SPEED Tooling costs are high and depend on the complexity of the design. Cycle time is between 30 and 60 seconds. Labour costs are relatively low. However, manual operations, such as mold preparation and demolding, increase the costs.

MATERIALS Most thermoplastic materials can be injection molded. It is also possible to mold certain thermosetting plastics, metal powders (see metal injection molding, page 48) and ceramic powders.

ENVIRONMENTAL IMPACTS Thermoplastic scrap can be directly recycled in this process. Up to 50% recycled material can be used in some applications, whereas medical products and food packaging require a higher level of virgin material.

Digital TV box fascias (above) Different-coloured versions are produced using the same molds and spray painted to achieve a high-quality finish. High gloss finish can be produced without spray painting, but this requires more expensive tooling.

Injection molded TV panel (right) It is possible to mold complex products in a single piece, from large car bumpers to the tiniest widgets. This TV panel has been injected in a single material and the front surface has been spray painted black and silver with a mask to achieve the designed colour contrast (see page 176).

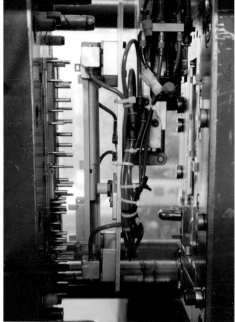

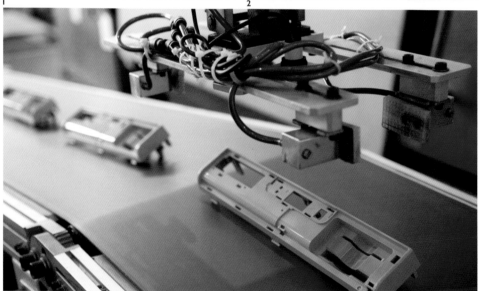

Case Study

Injection Molding a Digital TV Box

Featured company Young Sung Tis Co. Ltd
www.youngsungtis.co.kr

Injection molding consumer electronics is typically fully automated. The polymer is melted and mixed before injection into the die cavity. Once the die cavity has been filled, packed and clamped, and the polymer has resolidified, the two halves of the mold move apart (image **1**). The part is removed by a robotic arm and ejected from the mold by ejector pins (image **2**).

The part is placed onto a conveyer belt (image **3**) in preparation for spraying metallic silver (image **4**) and assembly (image **5**).

There are many parts that make up the digital TV box (image **6**). All of the plastic parts are injection molded.

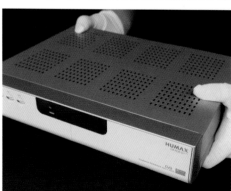

What is Gas-assisted Injection Molding?

Gas-assisted injection molding uses modified injection molding equipment. In stage one, plastic is injected into the mold cavity but does not completely fill it. In stage two, gas is injected and it forms a bubble in the molten plastic and forces it into the extremities of the mold. The plastic and gas injection cycles overlap. This produces a more even wall thickness because as more plastic is injected the air pressure pushes it through the mold like a viscous bubble. The gas bubble maintains equal pressure even over long and narrow profiles. Wall thickness can be 3 mm (0.118 in.) or more.

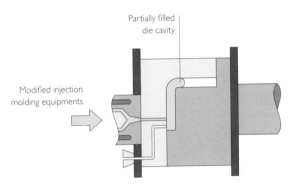

Partially filled die cavity

Modified injection molding equipments

Stage 1: Injection molding

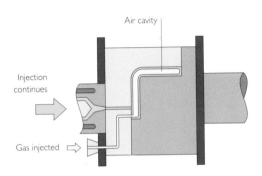

Air cavity

Injection continues

Gas injected

Stage 2: Gas injected

Gas-assisted injection molding sample This sample, cut from the leg of a Magis Air-Table, shows two technologies. The first is gas injection which creates the hollow profile. The second technology is the thin skin around the outside: there is a clear division between the outer unfilled polypropylene (PP) and the glass-filled structural PP. Two materials are used because the outer skin is aesthetic and therefore should not be filled. However, unfilled PP is not strong enough to make the entire structure.

Magis Air-Chair The Air-Chair was designed by Jasper Morrison and production began in Italy in 2000.

1

2

3

Case Study

Gas-assisted Injection Molding the Magis Air-Chair

Featured company Magis www.magisdesign.com

The gas-assisted injection molding sequence takes approximately three minutes. Polypropylene (PP) is injected into a two-part mold (image **1**), followed by an injection of gas which forms a bubble of air within the molten PP. This pushes the PP further into the die cavity without breaching it. After cooling, the molds separate, the chair is removed (image **2**) and placed onto a conveyor belt (image **3**).

The gas injection molding technique produces a plastic chair with a very good surface finish (image **4**). It weighs only 4.5 kg (9.92 lb) and can withstand heavy use.

4

What is Multishot Injection Molding?

Injection molding two or more plastics together is known as multishot or over-molding. It is possible to multishot up to six different materials simultaneously. It is known as 2K when two materials are combined, 3K for three materials and so on.

In stage one, polymers A and B are injected at the same time into different die cavities. The molten polymers form a strong bond because they are fused together under pressure.

In stage two, the molds separate and the sprue is removed from molded polymer A. Meanwhile the finished molding is ejected from the upper die cavity. The rotating platen spins to align molded polymer A with the upper die cavity and the process is repeated.

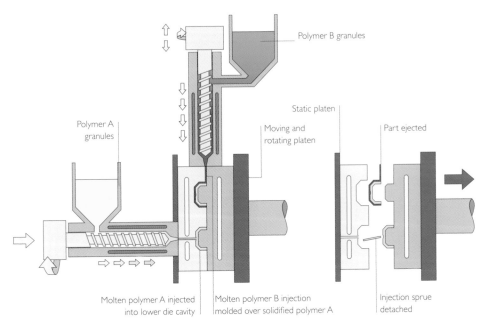

Polymer B granules

Static platen

Polymer A granules

Moving and rotating platen

Part ejected

Molten polymer A injected into lower die cavity

Molten polymer B injection molded over solidified polymer A

Injection sprue detached

Stage 1: Injection

Stage 2: Ejection

2K injection molded mobile phones These parts are typically molded in rigid polycarbonate (PC) or acrylonitrile butadiene styrene (ABS) with a flexible thermoplastic elastomer (TPE). The features of these materials are combined by multishot injection molding. The PC and ABS give the product rigidity, toughness and impact resistance. The TPE provides integral features with hermetic seals, such as buttons, and further improves impact resistance.

Case Study

2K Injection Molding a Soft Grip Tootbrush

Featured company Taekwang Techno Co. Ltd
www.tkmold.co.kr

The two injection sequences occur simultaneously: the lower die cavity is filled with rigid coloured polypropylene (PP) and the upper die cavity, which contains an already molded PP part, is over-molded with flexible white thermoplastic elastomer (TPE) (image **1**). The finished parts are removed from the upper die cavity (image **2**) and the mold is rotated through 180° (image **3**). In doing so, it brings the solidified PP into alignment with the second injection cavity.

Finished parts are packed for shipping (image **4**). It is possible to change the colour of either material to create a wide range of products.

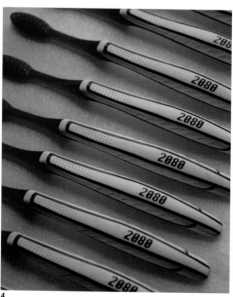

What is In-mold Decoration?

The in-mold decoration process is used to apply graphics to products during injection molding, thus eliminating secondary operations such as printing and spraying. It is also known as in-mold labelling (IML) and in-mold film (IMF), depending on the application and technique.

The process is used in the production of mobile phones, cameras, laptops and other injection molded products.

In stage one, a printed film – polycarbonate (PC), poly methyl methacrylate (PMMA), polyethylene terephthalate (PET) or even fabrics and veneers – is loaded into the die cavity prior to injection molding.

In stage two, when the hot plastic is injected in the die cavity it bonds with the film. The film becomes integral with the injection molded plastic, has a seamless finish and is an exact replica of the mold face.

If the surface of the mold is curved or patterned then the film is thermoformed to fit.

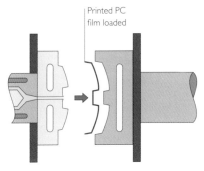

Printed PC film loaded

Stage 1: Film inserted

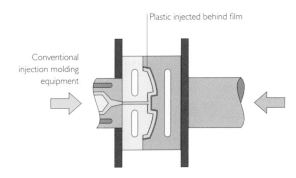

Conventional injection molding equipment

Plastic injected behind film

Stage 2: Conventional injection molding

Luceplan Lightdisc The Luceplan Lightdisc was designed by Alberto Meda and Paolo Rizzatto in 2002. By incorporating in-mold decoration, the diffuser acts as shade as well.

1

Case Study

In-mold Decoration Luceplan Lightdiscs

Featured company Luceplan www.luceplan.com

Graphics and instructions are included on the in-mold film (image **1**) and this eliminates all secondary printing. The film is prepared and placed into the mold by hand (image **2**).

The mold is clamped shut under 600 tonnes (661 US tons) of hydraulic pressure and the injection molding takes place (image **3**). The part is demolded (image **4**) and the finished molding is inspected prior to assembly (image **5**).

2

3

4

5

Metal Injection Molding

This process combines powder metallurgy with injection molding technology. It is used to manufacture small parts in steel, stainless steel, magnetic alloys, bronze, nickel alloys and cobalt alloys. A similar technique, known as powder injection molding, is used to shape ceramic materials and metal composites.

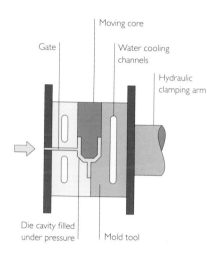

Stage 1: Injection molding

Gate

Moving core

Water cooling channels

Hydraulic clamping arm

Die cavity filled under pressure

Mold tool

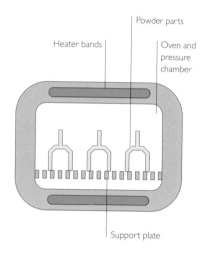

Stage 2: Heating and sintering

Powder parts

Heater bands

Oven and pressure chamber

Support plate

Essential Information

VISUAL QUALITY ●●●●●●●○○

SPEED ●●●●●●●○○

TOOLING COST ●●●●●●●○○

UNIT COST ●●●●○○○○○

ENVIRONMENT ●●●●●○○○○

Related processes include:
- Powder Injection Molding

Alternative and competing processes include:
- Centrifugal Casting
- Die Casting
- Investment Casting
- Rapid Prototyping
- Sand Casting

What is Metal Injection Molding?

Fine metal powder, typically no larger than 25 microns (0.00098 in.) in diameter, is compounded with around 20% thermoplastic and wax binder.

In stage one, the injection cycle is much the same as for other injection molding processes, although the molded parts are roughly 20% larger in every dimension prior to heating and sintering. This is to allow for the shrinkage.

In stage two, the 'green' parts are heated in an oven to vaporize and remove the thermoplastic and wax binder.

The final stage is to sinter the parts in a vacuum furnace. The 'green' part will shrink roughly 15–20% during sintering to accommodate the loss of material during debinding.

Notes for Designers

QUALITY Like injection molding, the high pressures used in this process ensure good surface finish, fine reproduction of detail and, most importantly, excellent repeatability.

TYPICAL APPLICATIONS The accuracy and speed of the process for manufacturing relatively small parts makes it ideal for manufacturing components for the aerospace, automotive and consumer electronics industries.

COST AND SPEED Tooling costs are high and depend on the complexity of design. Cycle time is between 30 and 60 seconds for the injection cycle. Removing the binder and sintering requires a further two to three days. Labour costs are relatively low.

MATERIALS Ferrous metals, including low-alloy steels, tool steels, stainless steels, magnetic alloys and bronze.

ENVIRONMENTAL IMPACTS Scrap material produced during the injection molding cycle can be directly recycled. Once the material has been sintered it cannot be recycled so readily, but rejects are rare at that stage because parts are accurate and repeatable.

Metal injection molding samples Metal injection molding combines the processing advantages of injection molding with the physical characteristics of metals. A wide range of geometries can be manufactured using this process, as demonstrated by these samples.

However, a significant consideration is the size of the part. The general size range is from 0.1 g to 100 g (0.0035–3.53 oz), or up to 150 mm (5.91 in.) in length. Such size restrictions relate to the sintering operation, which removes the plastic matrix and causes the part to shrink considerably. Large parts and thick wall sections are more likely to distort during the heating and sintering process.

Case Study

Metal Injection Molding a Cog

Featured company Metal Injection Mouldings Ltd
www.metalinjection.co.uk

The compounded metal powder and thermoplastic and wax binder are formed into pellets for injection molding (image **1**). The injection molding equipment is similar to that used for plastic injection molding (page 38) (image **2**).

The injection molded parts are a dull greyish colour – which is referred to as 'green' state – and they are surprisingly heavy due to their high level of metal content. They are placed onto support trays which are stacked up in the debind oven (images **3** and **4**).

The binder is completely removed in the debind oven, then high temperature sintering causes the metal particles to fuse together. The finished parts are solid metal with very little porosity (image **5**).

Foam Molding

Liquid polyurethane resin (PUR) is injected into a mold where it reacts to form a foamed part. PUR foam can be very soft and flexible or rigid. The foam cell structure is either open or closed. Open-cell foams tend to be softer and are upholstered or covered.

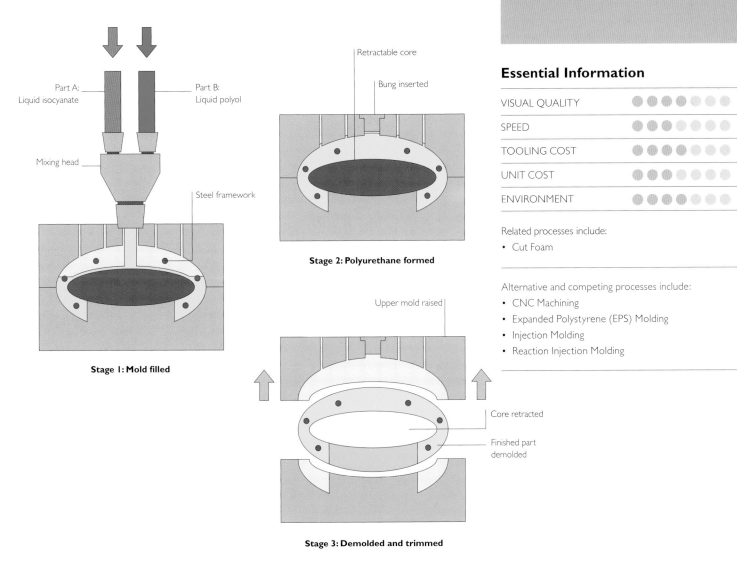

Part A:
Liquid isocyanate

Part B:
Liquid polyol

Mixing head

Steel framework

Stage 1: Mold filled

Retractable core

Bung inserted

Stage 2: Polyurethane formed

Upper mold raised

Core retracted

Finished part
demolded

Stage 3: Demolded and trimmed

Essential Information

VISUAL QUALITY	●●●●●○○○
SPEED	●●●●○○○○
TOOLING COST	●●●●●○○○
UNIT COST	●●●●○○○○
ENVIRONMENT	●●●●○○○○

Related processes include:
• Cut Foam

Alternative and competing processes include:
• CNC Machining
• Expanded Polystyrene (EPS) Molding
• Injection Molding
• Reaction Injection Molding

What is Cold Cure Foam Molding?

In stage one, the two ingredients that react to form polyurethane resin (PUR) foam, polyol and isocyanate are fed into the mixing head where they are combined at high pressure. The predetermined quantities of liquid chemicals are dispensed into the mold at a low pressure. As they are mixed they begin to go through a chemical exothermic reaction.

During stage two, the polymer expands to fill the mold. The only pressure on the mold is from the expanding liquid, so molds have to be designed and filled to ensure even spread of the polymer while it is still in its liquid state. In stage three, the product is demolded after five to 15 minutes.

Notes for Designers

QUALITY Even though this is a low-pressure process, the liquid PUR reproduces fine surface details well. The quality of the upholstery is largely dependent on the skill of the upholsterer.

TYPICAL APPLICATIONS All types of domestic and commercial furniture. PUR foam molding is also suitable for cushioning functions in footwear, such as in the soles, and for safety and tactility in toys.

COST AND SPEED Tooling costs are low to moderate. Cycle time is good. A typical mold will produce around 50 components per day. But the cost of upholstery is high due to the level of skill required.

MATERIALS Many types of plastics can be foamed. Upholstery materials suitable for high-wear applications include polyamide (PA) nylon, polyester, polyurethane, polyvinyl chloride (PVC), polyproylene (PP) and other hard-wearing fibres. General upholstery materials for low-wear applications include leather and cotton.

ENVIRONMENTAL IMPACTS Upholstered furniture is the culmination of many processes and as a consequence a typical sofa will include many different materials that have varying environmental implications. The isocyanates that are off gassed during the foam molding are harmful.

Case Study

Foam Molding the Eye Chair

Featured company Interfoam Limited
www.interfoam.co.uk

The Eye chair is molded in cold cure foam with a density of 55 kg/m^3 (3.4 lb/ft^3). The foam is supported by an internal metal structure which is over-molded (image **1**).

First of all the mold is prepared with a release agent (image **2**). The steelwork is loaded into the mold over the internal core and the whole assembly is closed and clamped shut. The two-part polymer is mixed and injected into the mold (image **3**). Once the reaction is complete the two halves of the mold are separated and the foamed part is removed (image **4**). The flash is trimmed and the part is ready to be assembled and upholstered (see page 159).

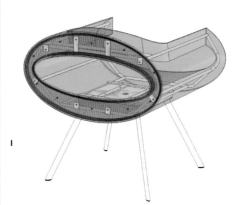

I

2

Expanding foam reaction (near right) A predetermined measure of polyol and isocyanate is dispensed into a plastic bag to demonstrate the reaction process.

The two liquids react and expand to form lightweight and flexible foam. The reaction is one way, so once the material has been formed it cannot be modified except by machining (page 112).

Self-skinning foam (far right) Polyurethane resin (PUR) is available in a range of densities, colours and hardnesses. It can be very soft and flexible (shore A range 25–90) or rigid (shore D range). The cell structure of foam materials is either open or closed. Open-cell foams tend to be softer and are upholstered or covered. Closed-cell foams are self-skinning and used in applications such as armrests with a faux leather imprint, for example (see far right).

3

4

Case Study

Upholstering with Cut Foam

Featured company Boss Design
www.boss-design.co.uk

This case study shows the upholstering
of the Neo chair using the cut-foam
technique. The structure is laminated wood
(image **1**) and the foam is bonded onto
it (images **2** and **3**). The covering material is
stretched over the foam and stapled onto
the plywood substrate. Each panel is made
up in this way and then fitted together
to conceal the inner workings of the chair.

1

3

2

Sona Chair An example of a foam-padded chair upholstered in the way described opposite is the Sona Chair, designed by Paul Brooks. Foam molding is more cost effective for complex and undulating shapes.

Range of foams There are many different types of foam, ranging from flexible to rigid, with either open or closed cells. The density, colour and hardness of foam can be specified to suit the requirements of the application.

Dip Molding

This low-cost method of producing thermoplastic products is used to make hollow and sheet geometries in flexible and semi-rigid materials. As a coating method, this process can build up a thick, bright, insulating and protective layer on metal parts.

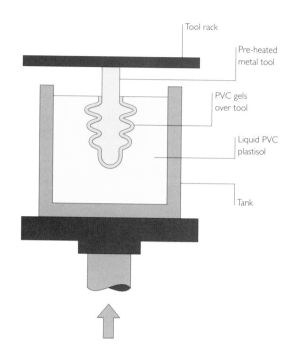

Tool rack

Pre-heated
metal tool

PVC gels
over tool

Liquid PVC
plastisol

Tank

Essential Information

VISUAL QUALITY	●●●●○○○○○
SPEED	●●●○○○○○○
TOOLING COST	●●●○○○○○○
UNIT COST	●●●●○○○○○
ENVIRONMENT	●●●●●○○○

Related processes include:
• Dip Coating

Alternative and competing processes include:
• Rotation Molding
• Spray Painting
• Thermoforming

What is Dip Molding?

The hot metal tool is coated with a dilute silicone solution for dip molding and with a primer for dip coating. The tank rises up to submerge the tool to the fill line. On contact, the plastisol gels to form polymerized polyvinyl chloride (PVC) on the tool surface. The wall thickness rapidly builds up, reaching 2.5 mm (0.1 in.) within 60 seconds. The PVC polymerizes at 60°C (140°F), so as the tool cools and the wall thickness builds up, polymerization slows down. Once the PVC has polymerized it cannot be returned to a liquid and so cannot be recycled directly.

QUALITY Dip molding and coating produce parts with a smooth and seamless finish. There is a single male tool and so there are no split lines, flash or other related imperfections. The outside surface (that does not come into contact with the tool) tends to be glossy.

TYPICAL APPLICATIONS A wide range of industries, including automotive, mining, marine, medical, aerospace, and promotion and marketing. Roughly 60% of dip molding is for electrical insulation covers, due to PVC's high electrical insulation properties.

COST AND SPEED Tooling costs are minimal. Cycle time is rapid and multiple tools reduce cycle time dramatically.

MATERIALS PVC is the most common material used for dip molding and coating. Other materials, including nylon, silicone, latex and urethane, are also used, but only for specialist applications.

ENVIRONMENTAL IMPACTS The environmental credibility of PVC has been under investigation in recent years due to dioxins, harmful organic compounds that are given off during both the production and the incineration of the material.

Vivid colours There are many vivid colours available and parts can be produced with gloss, matt or foam-like finishes. PVC is also available in clear, metallic, fluorescent and translucent grades.

1

2

Dip Molding a Flexible Bellow

Featured company Cove Industries
www.cove-industries.co.uk

The hot aluminium tools are dipped in dilute silicone solution. The tools are mounted above the tank of room temperature liquid plastisol PVC (image **1**). They are submerged steadily, ensuring that the viscous liquid does not fold over on itself and trap air (image **2**). After 45 seconds the tank is lowered to reveal the dip-molded parts (image **3**), which are quickly inverted (image **4**) and placed in an oven to cure fully.

The inside of the final part is matt (replicating the tool) and the outside is smooth and glossy (image **5**).

3

4

5

High Pressure Die Casting

High pressure die casting is a versatile process and the most rapid way of forming non-ferrous metal parts. High pressure forces molten metal into the mold to create precise, intricate and complex 3D geometries. It is widely used in the product, furniture and automotive industries.

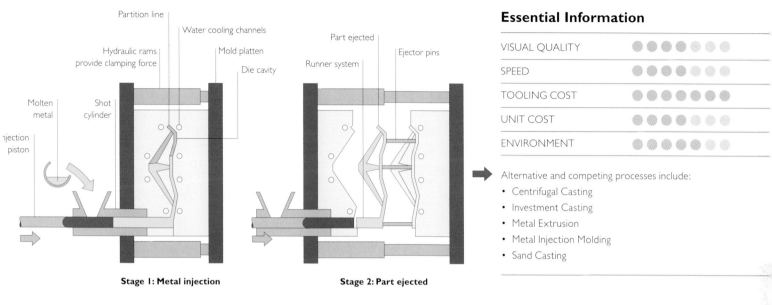

Stage 1: Metal injection

Stage 2: Part ejected

Labels (Stage 1):
Partition line
Water cooling channels
Hydraulic rams provide clamping force
Mold platten
Die cavity
Molten metal
Shot cylinder
Injection piston

Labels (Stage 2):
Part ejected
Ejector pins
Runner system

What is High Pressure Die Casting?

In stage one, the hot liquid metal is forced into the die cavity by the shot piston at high pressure. The pressure is maintained until the part has solidified. Water-cooling channels help to keep the mold temperature lower than the casting material and so accelerate cooling within the die cavity.

In stage two, when the parts are sufficiently cool, which can take anything from a few seconds to several minutes depending on size, the part is ejected. High pressure die-cast parts require very little machining or finishing because a very high surface finish can be achieved in the mold.

Notes for Designers

QUALITY Die-cast parts have a superior surface finish. Voids and porosity are an inevitable part of metal casting, as a result of turbulence in the flow of metal, which can be limited when engineering the product at the design stage.

TYPICAL APPLICATIONS High pressure die casting is used to produce the majority of die-cast metal parts such as for the automotive industry, white goods, consumer electronics, packaging, furniture, lighting, jewelry and toys.

COST AND SPEED The tooling and equipment is very expensive, and so this process is suitable only for high-volume production. Labour costs are low for automated die-casting methods.

MATERIALS Non-ferrous metals, including aluminium, magnesium, zinc, copper, lead and tin, are all suitable for die casting. Aluminium and magnesium have become popular for consumer electronics due to their high strength to weight properties. The surface of aluminium can be anodized (page 170). However, the surface porosity will impact on the quality of the finish.

ENVIRONMENTAL IMPACTS This process uses a great deal of energy to melt the alloys and maintain them at high temperatures for casting.

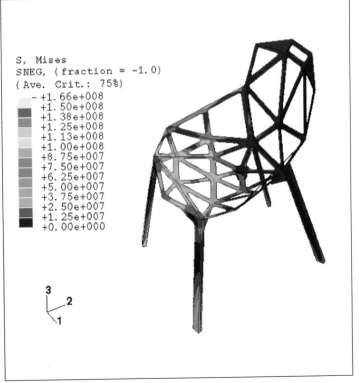

S, Mises
SNEG, (fraction = -1.0)
(Ave. Crit.: 75%)
- +1.66e+008
+1.50e+008
+1.38e+008
+1.25e+008
+1.13e+008
+1.00e+008
+8.75e+007
+7.50e+007
+6.25e+007
+5.00e+007
+3.75e+007
+2.50e+007
+1.25e+007
+0.00e+000

Virtual analysis of Magis Chair-One Strength analysis of Magis Chair-One shows the resilience of the structure. This software is used to double check that the engineering of the product is correct before manufacturing the tools for casting.

1

High Pressure Die Casting Magis Chair-One

Featured company Magis www.magisdesign.com

Chair-One was designed by Konstantin Grcic for Magis in 2001 and took three years to develop for production (image **1**).

The raw material (which may come from recycled stock) is melted in a furnace (image **2**). It is collected in a crucible and poured into the shot cylinder (image **3**) and injected into the die cavity.

After two minutes the molds separate to reveal the solidified part, which is collected by a robotic arm (image **4**). The part is cooled in water, and the flash and runner systems are removed (image **5**).

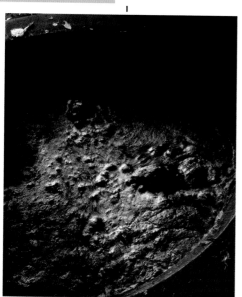

2

3

4

5

Investment Casting

This is an expensive metal-casting process, but the opportunities far outweigh the cost implications for many applications. Liquid metals are formed into complex and intricate shapes in this process, which uses non-permanent ceramic molds. It is also known as lost wax casting.

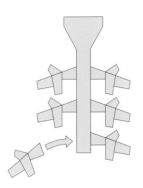

Stage 1: Assemble wax patterns onto tree

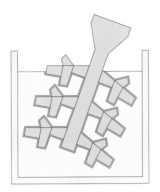

Stage 2: Assembly coated in ceramic slurry

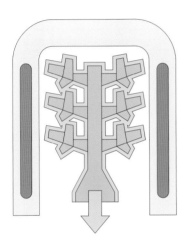

Stage 3: Wax melted out and ceramic mold fired

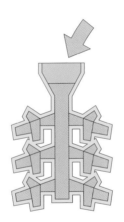

Stage 4: Metal poured into hot mold

What is Investment Casting?

In stage one, the expendable patterns are formed and assembled together on a central-feed system. In stage two, it is dipped in ceramic slurry and then coated with fine grains of refractory material by spraying.

In stage three, the wax patterns and runner system are melted out in a steam autoclave and the ceramic shell is subsequently fired at 1095°C (2003°F).

In stage four, molten metal is poured in. Once the casting has solidified and cooled, it is broken out of the shell mold.

The parts are removed from the central feed system, fettled, abrasive blasted and heat-treated to improve the physical properties of the material.

Notes for Designers

QUALITY Investment casting produces high-integrity metal parts with superior metallurgical properties. The surface finish is generally very good.

TYPICAL APPLICATIONS Application examples include gears, housings, electronic chassis, covers and fascias, engine parts, turbine blades, medical implants, brackets, levers and handles.

COST AND SPEED There are moderate tooling costs for the wax-injection process. Cycle time is long and generally 24 hours or more. Labour costs can be quite high.

MATERIALS The most commonly cast materials are carbon and low-alloy steels, stainless steels, aluminium, titanium, zinc, copper alloys and precious metals. Nickel, cobalt and magnetic alloys are also cast.

ENVIRONMENTAL IMPACTS Very little waste is produced that cannot be recycled. However, this is an energy intensive process.

Case Study

Investment Casting a Consumer Electronic Housing

Featured company PI Castings
www.pi-castings.co.uk

This is the production of a liquid sample testing device used in the medical industry (image **1**). The expendable pattern is injection molded wax (image **2**). The mold tool is slightly larger than the final part to allow for shrinkage. The patterns are assembled onto a runner system and dipped into a water-based zircon ceramic solution (image **3**). The thickness of coating is built up in layers. The wax is removed in a steam autoclave (image **4**). The hollow ceramic shell is placed in a kiln at 1095°C (2003°F) to harden it fully and remove any residual wax.

The aluminium alloy is heated to 710°C (1310°F) and poured into the hot mold (image **5**). Once it has cooled, the ceramic shell is broken from the solidified metal parts (image **6**).

1

2

3

Investment-cast part (near right) Investment casting does not have the same shape limitations as other casting techniques, so it is possible to cast shapes with undercuts and varying wall thickness. This eliminates costly fabrication or machining operations.

Rapid prototyped wax pattern (far right) A range of material and forming processes are utilized in the production of the pattern (over which the ceramic shell mold is formed) for prototypes and low volumes. Rapid prototyping techniques include selective laser sintering (SLS), stereolithography (SLA) and thermojet wax (pictured). The design of the part will determine the most suitable process.

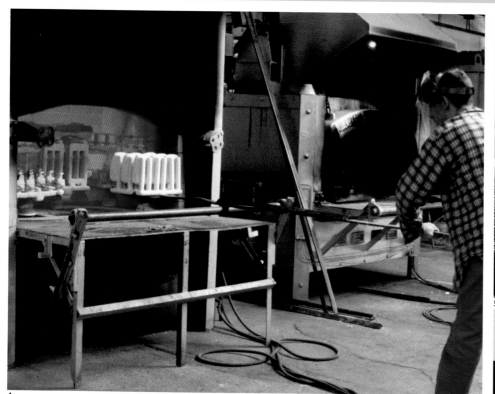

4

5

6

Metal Press Forming

In these sheet-metal forming processes the part is made by a punch that forces the metal blank into a closely matched die. Shallow parts are formed by stamping and very deep profiles can be formed using progressive dies in a process known as deep drawing.

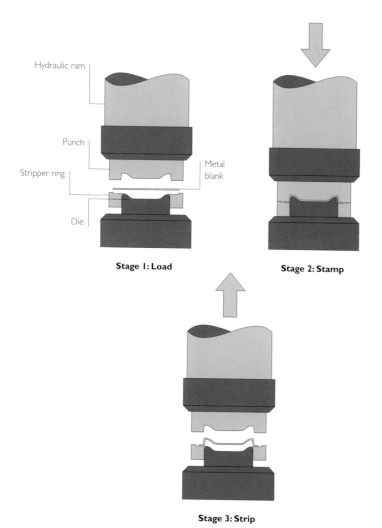

Hydraulic ram

Punch

Stripper ring

Die

Metal blank

Stage 1: Load

Stage 2: Stamp

Stage 3: Strip

Essential Information

VISUAL QUALITY	●●●●●●○
SPEED	●●●●●○○○
TOOLING COST	●●●●●○○○
UNIT COST	●●●●○○○○
ENVIRONMENT	●●●●○○○

Related processes include:
- Deep Drawing
- Metal Stamping

Alternative and competing processes include:
- Metal Spinning
- Panel Beating
- Press Braking
- Superplastic Forming

What is Metal Stamping?

Metal stamping is carried out on a punch press. The punch and die (matched tooling) are dedicated and generally carry out a single operation such as forming or punching. In operation, the metal blank is loaded onto the stripper. The punch then clamps and forms the part in a single stroke.

After forming, the stripper rises up to eject the part, which is removed. Sometimes the part is formed in a continuous strip, and many sheet-metal processes are carried out in sequence to form the part (see page 74). This is the norm in very high-volume production.

QUALITY Shaped metal profiles combine the ductility and strength of metals in parts with improved rigidity and lightness. Surface finish is generally very good.

TYPICAL APPLICATIONS A wide range of products, including camera bodies, mobile phones, kitchenware, office equipment, kitchen sinks and products for the automotive and aerospace industries.

COST AND SPEED Tooling costs are high because tools have to be extremely precise. Progressive tooling, required to produce complex or especially deep parts, increases costs considerably. Cycle time is rapid and ranges from one to over 100 parts per minute.

MATERIALS Shallow profiles can be formed in carbon steel, stainless steel, aluminium, magnesium, titanium, copper, brass and zinc. Deeper profiles rely on a combination of a metal's malleability and resistance to thinning. The most suitable materials are steels, zinc, copper and aluminium alloys.

ENVIRONMENTAL IMPACTS There is no heat required during this process and all scrap can be recycled.

Alessi Mediterraneo Bowl Parts with a complex profile are cut prior to forming. The Mediterraneo Bowl, designed by Emma Silvestris in 2005, is laser cut. Very high volumes tend to be punched and blanked (page 76).

 The thickness of stainless steel that can be stamped is generally between 0.4 mm and 2 mm (0.02–0.08 in.). It is possible to stamp thicker sheet, up to 6 mm (0.236 in.), but this will affect the shape that can be formed.

Case Study

Metal Stamping the Alessi Serving Tray

Featured company Alessi www.alessi.com

Alessi is an example of a manufacturer that uses metal pressing to produce parts of the highest standard. The example here is a serving plate which is formed in stainless steel sheet. It was designed by Jasper Morrison in 2000 (image **1**). The blank is loaded onto the tool and stamped (images **2–4**). It is a rapid process and each part takes only a few seconds to complete. The part is removed from the stripper (image **5**), trimmed and polished.

What is Deep Drawing?

The deep drawing process is carried out in different ways – the method of process being determined by the complexity of the shape, depth of draw, material and thickness. In stage one, a sheet-metal blank is loaded into the hydraulic press and clamped into the blank holder. In stage two, as the blank holder progresses downwards the material flows over the sides of the lower die to form a symmetrical cup shape. In stage three, the punch forces the material through the lower die in the opposite direction. This is known as 'reverse deep drawing'. In stage four, the part is ejected.

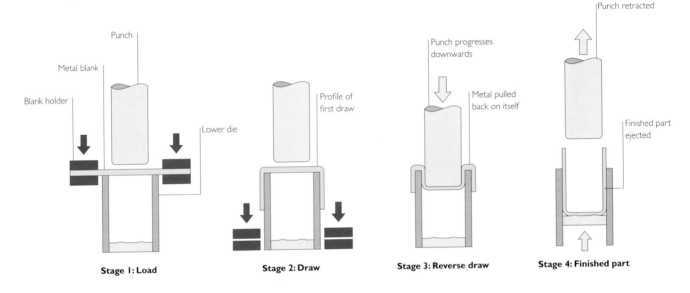

Stage 1: Load

Stage 2: Draw

Stage 3: Reverse draw

Stage 4: Finished part

Mass production with progressive dies Parts manufactured in very high volumes that require multiple forming and cutting operations are produced with progressive dies, a process made up of a series of dies working very rapidly and in tandem. While a part is being formed the second operation is being carried out simultaneously on the part that was formed previously and so on. Parts may require five operations or more, which is reflected in the number of workstations. The process is fully automated and the parts are moved between the workstations by a transfer yoke.

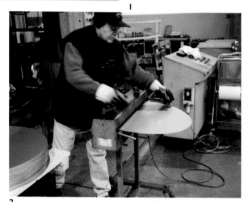

1

2

3

Case Study

Deep Drawing the Cribbio

Featured company Rexite www.rexite.it

The Rexite Cribbio is epoxy-coated carbon steel (image **1**). It begins as a circular metal blank which is 0.8 mm (0.031 in.) thick (image **2**). The final part has a reduced wall thickness of 0.7 mm (0.028 in.) as a result of thinning during drawing.

The metal is forced to flow over the lower die by a 500 tonne press (image **3**). The drawn part is loaded onto the second of the progressive dies. A punch forces the material into the lower die, turning it inside out, to form the final profile (image **4**). Finishing includes trimming, punching (image **5**) and epoxy coating.

4

5

Punching and Blanking

In this process, circular, square and profiled holes can be cut from sheet materials using a hardened steel punch. Tooling is either dedicated or interchangeable, depending on the geometry and complexity of design.

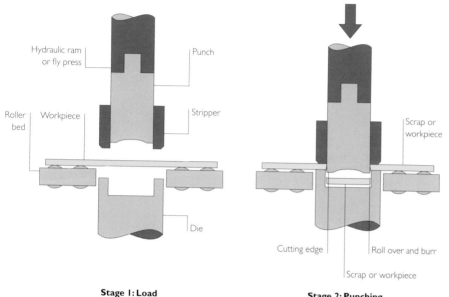

Hydraulic ram or fly press

Punch

Roller bed

Workpiece

Stripper

Die

Stage 1: Load

Scrap or workpiece

Cutting edge

Roll over and burr

Scrap or workpiece

Stage 2: Punching

Essential Information

VISUAL QUALITY	●●●●○○○○○
SPEED	●●●●●●○○○
TOOLING COST	●●●●●○○○○
UNIT COST	●●●○○○○○○
ENVIRONMENT	●●●○○○○○○

Alternative and competing processes include:

- CNC Turret Punching
- Laser Cutting
- Photochemical Machining
- Water Jet Cutting

What is Punching and Blanking?

It is possible to punch a single hole, multiple holes simultaneously, or many holes with the same punch. In stage one, the workpiece is loaded onto the roller bed. In stage two, the stripper and die clamp the workpiece. The hardened punch stamps through it, causing the metal to fracture between the circumferences of the punch and die.

Once cut, the punch retracts and the stripper ensures that the metal comes free. Either the punched material or the surrounding material is scrap, depending on whether it is a punching or blanking operation. In both cases the scrap is collected and recycled.

QUALITY The shearing action is precise and highly repeatable. Punching tends to be used to add function to a metal part such as perforations or fixing points. It is also used for decorative applications because a punched hole can be any shape the designer chooses. The shearing action forms 'roll over' on the cut edges. This results in burrs, which are sharp and have to be removed by grinding and polishing.

TYPICAL APPLICATIONS Some typical products include kitchenware, such as colanders, bowls and plates, consumer electronic and appliance enclosures, general metalwork and automotive body parts.

COST AND SPEED Standard and small tools are inexpensive. Specialized and 3D tools are more expensive. Cycle time is rapid. Between one and 100 punches can be made every minute.

MATERIALS Almost all metals can be processed in this way including carbon steel, stainless steel and aluminium and copper alloys. Other materials, including leather, textiles, plastic, paper and card, can also be punched. Punching in this case is typically referred to as die cutting.

ENVIRONMENTAL IMPACTS Parts can be nested very efficiently on a sheet to minimize scrap. Any scrap is collected and separated for recycling, so there is very little wasted material.

Blanked Alessi characters Punching and blanking are essentially the same, but the names indicate different uses: punching refers to cutting an internal shape and blanking is cutting an external shape in a single operation. For example, these figures are blanked from Alessi stainless steel products and leave a punched hole of exactly the same shape.

Punching the Alessi Tralcio Muto Tray

Featured company Alessi www.alessi.com

This case study illustrates a stage in the production of the Tralcio Muto tray, which was designed for Alessi by Marta Sansoni in 2000. The tray is press formed (page 70) in stainless steel; the edges are trimmed, de-burred and rolled. The part is coated in a thin film of oil (image **1**) and loaded one at a time into the dedicated tool (image **2**). The design is such that the punching operation is carried out in two stages. The first punch is made (image **3**) and the product is rotated through 90° and punched again to produce the complete pattern (image **4**).

2

3

4

Metal Spinning

Spinning is a sheet-metal forming process used in the manufacture of rotationally symmetrical parts such as cylinders, cones and hemispheres. It is carried out on a single-sided tool, as progressive tooling or – in a process known as spinning 'on-air' – without tooling at all.

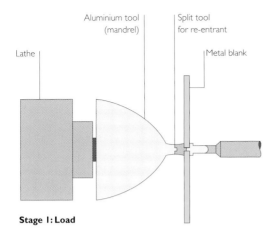

Lathe

Aluminium tool
(mandrel)

Split tool
for re-entrant

Metal blank

Stage 1: Load

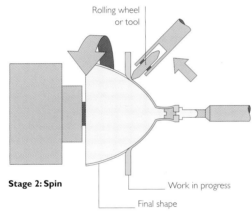

Rolling wheel
or tool

Stage 2: Spin

Work in progress

Final shape

Essential Information

VISUAL QUALITY	●●●●●○○○
SPEED	●●●○○○○○
TOOLING COST	●●●●○○○○
UNIT COST	●●●●●●○○
ENVIRONMENT	●●●●○○○○

Related processes include:
• On-air (without tool)
• Progressive Tool
• Single-sided Tool

Alternative and competing processes include:
• Metal Press Forming
• Panel Beating
• Superplastic Forming

What is Metal Spinning?

In stage one of the spinning process a circular metal blank is loaded onto the tool (mandrel). In stage two, the metal blank and mandrel are spun on the lathe and a rolling wheel forces the metal sheet onto the surface of the mandrel. This stage of the process is similar to throwing clay on a potter's wheel. The metal is gradually shaped and thinned as it is pressed onto the mandrel.

In this case the finished part cannot be removed from the mandrel until it is trimmed because there is a re-entrant angle. The whole process takes less than a minute.

Notes for Designers

QUALITY A very high finish is achievable. Manual and automated techniques are often combined for optimum quality. Textures can be integrated onto only one side of the part because a low-profile texture on the mold will not be visible on the opposite surface.

TYPICAL APPLICATIONS Some typical products made in this way include anglepoise lampshades, lamp stands, flanged caps and covers, clock façades, bowls and dishes.

COST AND SPEED For large production runs the metal tooling costs are considerably cheaper than for metal stamping and deep drawing because metal spinning uses a single-sided tool. Spinning 'on-air' needs no tooling, but the labour costs tend to be higher.

MATERIALS Mild steel, stainless steel, brass, copper, aluminium and titanium can all be formed by metal spinning.

ENVIRONMENTAL IMPACTS Energy requirements for this process are quite low, especially if it is manually operated. The energy used is equivalent to turning a lathe.

Metal spinning undercuts Metal spinning is limited to rotationally symmetrical parts. The ideal shape for this process is a hemisphere, where the diameter is greater than or equal to twice the depth. Parallel sides and re-entrant angles are possible with a split tool.

1

Case Study

Spinning the Grito Lampshade

Featured company Mathmos www.mathmos.co.uk

The Grito Lampshade was designed by El Ultimo Grito for Mathmos (image **1**).

The metal blank is cut and loaded onto the mandrel and the CNC metal rolling wheel guides the blank over the surface of the mandrel in stages (image **2**). It takes only 30 seconds to complete the first stage of the spinning process (image **3**).

In this case a second manual spinning operation is required to achieve a re-entrant angle on the neck of the lampshade (image **4**).

After spinning, the shade is punched (image **5**), anodized outside and painted inside.

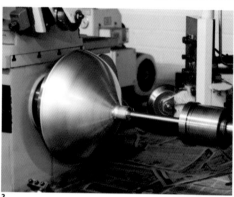

2

3

4

5

Tube and Section Bending

Used mainly in the furniture, automotive and construction industries, this process is used to form continuous and fluid metal structures. Tight bends can be formed with a mandrel over a rotating die, or long and undulating curves between rollers.

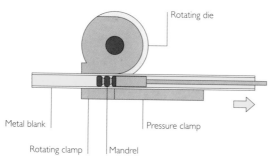

Rotating die

Metal blank

Rotating clamp | Mandrel

Pressure clamp

Stage 1: Load

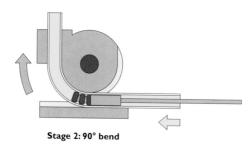

Stage 2: 90° bend

Essential Information

VISUAL QUALITY	●●●●●○○
SPEED	●●●●●○○
TOOLING COST	●●○○○○○
UNIT COST	●●●●○○○
ENVIRONMENT	●●●○○○○

Related processes include:
- Mandrel Bending
- Ring Rolling

Alternative and competing processes include:
- Press Braking
- Swaging

What is Mandrel Bending?

The metal blank (tube) is loaded over the mandrel and clamped onto the die. Non-mandrel forming is only possible for certain parts with thicker walls.

The blank is drawn onto the rotating die as it turns, and the mandrel stops the walls collapsing at the point of bending. The pressure clamp travels with the tube to maintain an accurate and wrinkle-free bend. An additional clamp is sometimes required to prevent wrinkling on the inside of the bend, especially for very thin walled sections.

The size of the rotating die determines the radius of the bend. The distance travelled determines the angle of bend.

Notes for Designers

QUALITY Applying a bend to a sheet of material increases its strength; these processes combine the ductility and strength of metals to produce parts with improved rigidity and lightness.

TYPICAL APPLICATIONS A range of products including furniture, security fencing and automotive applications (such as exhaust pipes). It is possible to produce 3D section bends, such as the tracks on a rollercoaster, by ring rolling.

COST AND SPEED Standard tooling is used to produce a wide range of bent geometries. Specialized tooling will increase the unit price considerably, but will depend on the size and complexity of the bend. Cycle time is rapid in most operations.

MATERIALS Almost all metals can be formed in this way including steel, aluminium, copper and titanium. Ductile metals will bend more easily.

ENVIRONMENTAL IMPACTS Bending, as opposed to cutting and welding, is generally less wasteful and a more efficient use of energy. There is no scrap produced in the bending operation.

Case Study

Mandrel Bending the S 43 Chair

Featured company Thonet www.thonet.de

Mart Stam designed the S 43 Chair (image **1**), which was introduced by Thonet in 1931.

The steel tube (image **2**) is loaded over the mandrel and into the pressure clamps (image **3**). The CNC machine aligns the tube and the bending sequence begins. The operation is precisely controlled and there is no scrap; the bending process uses the entire length of tube (image **4**).

The laminated wood seat and back are assembled onto the bent tube structure with rivets (image **5**). The final product is simple, lightweight and uses the minimum material.

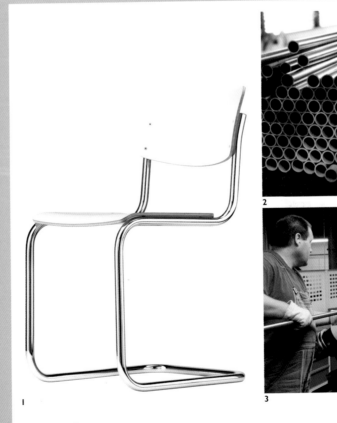

1

2

3

Thonet S 5000 The modular S 5000 furniture series was designed by James Irvine for Thonet and production began in 2006. Mandrel bending has been used here to produce the base structure, which enables the top components – back rest and arm rests – to be interchanged.

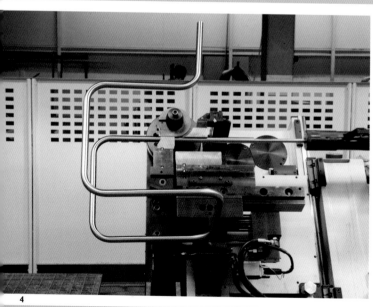

4

5

What is Ring Rolling?

Ring rolling is much simpler than mandrel bending in operation. The tube, profile or sheet is passed between three rollers. One of the rollers, in this case the bottom right, is moved inwards to make the bend tighter. The radius of the bend is decreased gradually over several cycles to avoid cracking or wrinkling the metal. The blank is rolled back and forth until the curve becomes the required shape.

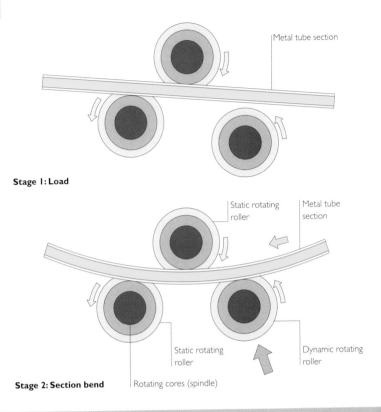

Stage 1: Load

Metal tube section

Static rotating roller

Metal tube section

Static rotating roller

Dynamic rotating roller

Stage 2: Section bend

Rotating cores (spindle)

Thonet S 826 (below) Ulrich Böhme designed the S 826 rocking chair for Thonet in 1971. The radius of the bent metal structure is not constant; this process can be used to produce arcs that do not fit into a circle.

Ring rolling heating elements (right) Continuous circular metal profiles, such as these heating elements, are produced by ring rolling and then arc welding the seam.

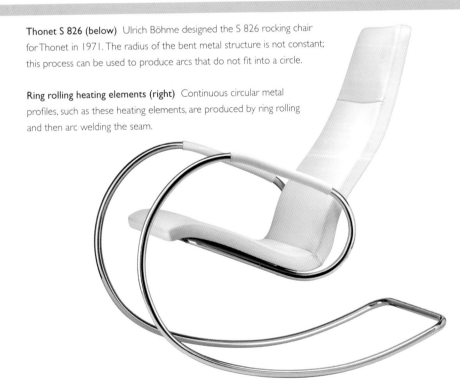

Case Study

Ring Rolling

Featured company Pipecraft www.pipecraft.co.uk

In this process metal tube is cut to length (image **1**) and fed into the rollers. The rollers are adjusted to bend the pipe gradually into the desired radius (image **2**). As the rollers move closer together the radius of the bend will be decreased. These are parts of a larger structure and do not require a tight radius (image **3**). In this case the process is being used to bend tubular steel; a range of profiles and flat sections can be bent, but require rollers with fitting profiles.

1

2

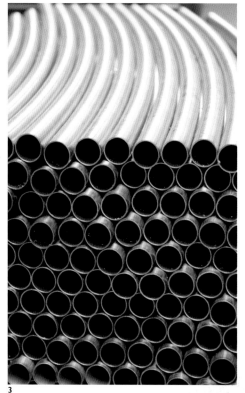

3

Swaging

Swaging is the manipulation of metal tube, rod or wire in a die. It is used to reduce cross section by drawing out the material and expanding the diameter of pipe by stretching into tapers, joints or sealed ends. There are two swaging techniques: hammering and pressing.

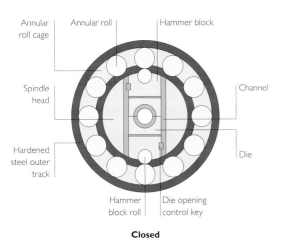

Annular roll cage | Annular roll | Hammer block

Spindle head

Channel

Hardened steel outer track

Die

Hammer block roll | Die opening control key

Closed

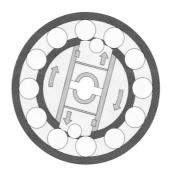

Open

What is Rotary Swaging?

In rotary swaging the metal is manipulated by a hammering action. This is generated by hammer blocks, which move in and out on the hammer block roll as the spindle head rotates rapidly.

The die opening, which is at its full extent when the spindle head rotates and the hammer block rolls fall between the annular rolls, determines the size of the tube that can be swaged.

Notes for Designers

QUALITY Swaging compresses or expands metal during the operation. Steel work hardens in these conditions, which improves its mechanical properties. The surface finish is generally very good and can be improved with polishing.

TYPICAL APPLICATIONS Swaging is used to form large parts such as cylindrical lamp posts, connectors and joints for load-bearing cables, and piping for gas and water. It is also widely employed for small and precise products such as ammunition casing, electrodes for welding torches and thermometer probes.

COST AND SPEED Tooling is generally inexpensive, but depends on the length and complexity of the swage. Cycle time is rapid.

MATERIALS Almost all metals can be formed in this way including steel, aluminium, copper, brass and titanium. Ductile metals will swage more easily.

ENVIRONMENTAL IMPACTS Swaging is not a reductive process like machining. In fact, the hammering or pressing action can strengthen the metal blank, contributing towards a longer lasting product.

Rotary swaging is generally a manually operated process. The vibration can cause 'white finger', especially in larger parts.

Rotary swaged probe Rotary swaging is capable of forming not only open-ended tapers, but also sealed ends in a length of pipe. This is especially useful for hollow probes and spikes.

This 25 mm (0.98 in.) diameter tube has been formed into a 30° taper to a sealed end: the last 10 mm (0.4 in.) is solid metal.

Case Study

Rotary Swaging Steel Tube

Featured company Elmill Group www.elmill.com

In this case, steel tube is being formed into a taper with an open end (image **1**). The pipe is forced into the swaging die as it rotates at high speed (image **2**). After 20 seconds or so, the pipe is retracted fully formed (image **3**). The last 10 mm (0.4 in.) is likely to be solid metal. The diameter of the hole at the end can be made precise by swaging the pipe over metal wire.

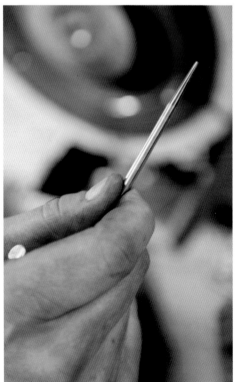

What is Hydraulic Swaging?

In hydraulic swaging the pressure is applied to either the inside or the outside of the pipe diameter. It is typically applied simultaneously, from at least five die segments which surround the pipe wall. Turning the pipe during forming ensures even deformation of the wall section.

The hydraulic action is applied along the axis of the pipe being formed. The guide block is wedge shaped and forces the die to either contract or expand. The die determines the shape and angle of swage, which can be parallel or tapered.

For parallel end forming, such as joint forming, standard tools are available for each pipe diameter. Tapered swaging requires specially designed tooling.

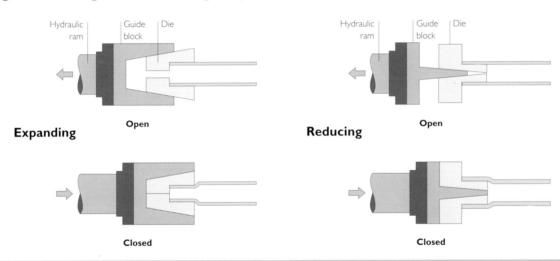

Expanding

Hydraulic ram | Guide block | Die

Open

Closed

Reducing

Hydraulic ram | Guide block | Die

Open

Closed

Case Study

Hydraulic Swaging

Featured company Pipecraft www.pipecraft.co.uk

Swaging dies are used either to expand the diameter of a pipe (images **1, 2** and **3**) or to reduce it (images **4, 5** and **6**). The part is continuously rotated during operation to produce a uniform finish. Hydraulic swaging can be applied to a variety of profiles, including square and triangular sections as well as round.

1

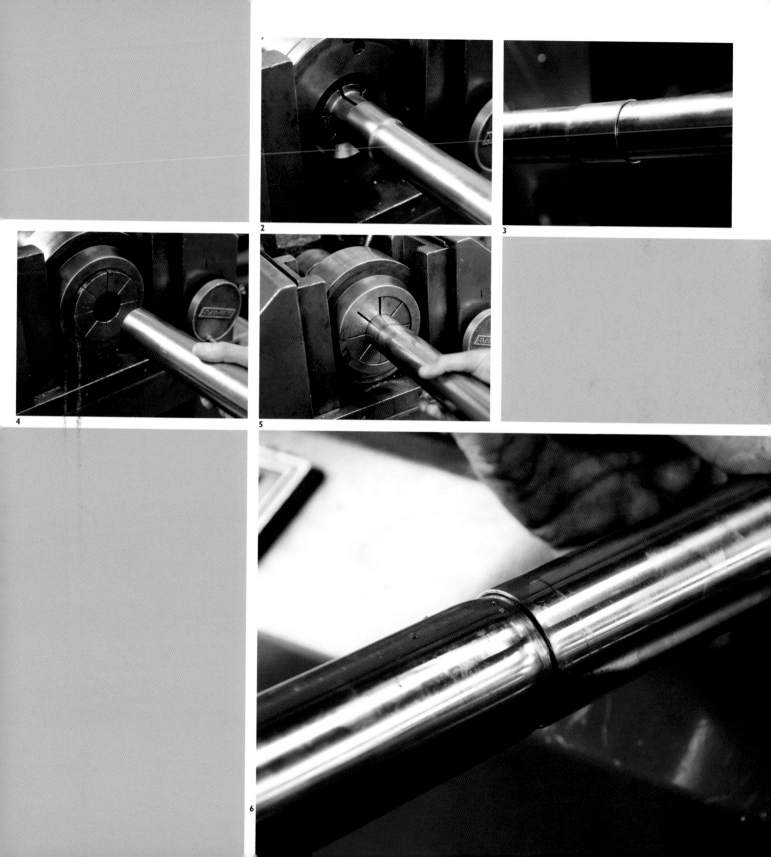

2

3

4

5

6

Superplastic Forming

This recently developed hot forming process is used to produce sheet-metal parts following similar principles to plastic thermoforming: a metal blank is heated and formed using air pressure. This process relies on the superplastic properties of specific grades of aluminium, titanium and magnesium.

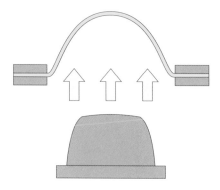

Stage 1: Pre-heated sheet loaded and blown

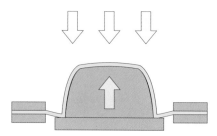

Stage 2: Vacuum applied

Essential Information

VISUAL QUALITY	●●●●●●○○
SPEED	●●●●●○○○
TOOLING COST	●●●●●●○○
UNIT COST	●●●●●●○○
ENVIRONMENT	●●●●●○○○

Related processes include:
• Back Pressure Forming
• Bubble Forming
• Cavity Forming
• Diaphragm Forming

Alternative and competing processes include:
• Metal Press Forming
• Metal Spinning
• Panel Beating

What is Superplastic Forming?

There are four main superplastic forming techniques: cavity, bubble, back pressure and diaphragm. In all four processes a sheet of metal is loaded into the machine, clamped in place and heated to between 450°C and 500°C (840–932°F). The temperature is determined by the type and thickness of the sheet material.

Bubble forming is similar to thermoforming (page 22). In stage one, the hot metal sheet is blown into a bubble and the tool rises into the mold chamber. In stage two, the pressure is then reversed and the bubble of metal is forced onto the outside surface of the tool. This process is ideal for deep and complex parts. The wall thickness is uniform because the bubble process stretches the material evenly.

Notes for Designers

QUALITY Like thermoforming, the side of the sheet that does not come into contact with the mold will have the highest quality finish. The compatible materials exhibit good corrosion resistance, mechanical strength and surface finish.

TYPICAL APPLICATIONS Examples of superplastic forming can be found in aerospace, automotive, buildings, trains, electronics, furniture and sculpture.

COST AND SPEED Although tooling costs are lower than for metal press forming, the total cost and cycle time depends on the size and complexity of the part. Cycle time is rapid, typically five to 20 minutes.

MATERIALS Superplastic metals that can be shaped in this manner include aluminium, magnesium and titanium alloys. The most commonly formed aluminium sheet materials include 5083, 2004 and 7475.

ENVIRONMENTAL IMPACTS Scrap and offcuts are recycled to produce new sheets of aluminium and other aluminium products. A lot of heat is required to raise the temperature of the tool and metal blank during processing.

Biomega MN01 bike Since its conception in the 1970s, superplastic forming has had a major impact on the automotive, aerospace, construction and rail industries because complex 3D shapes can be produced from a single sheet of material. Recently, designers such as Marc Newson have begun to explore the possibilities of using this technology to produce consumer products, for instance, bicycles.

Superplastic aluminium samples Tests show that a piece of superplastic aluminium alloy will stretch several times its length without breaking. This contrasts with standard types which fracture more readily when stretched.

1

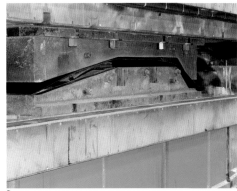

3

Case Study

Superplastic Forming the Siemens Desiro Train Façade

Featured company Superform Aluminium
www.superform-aluminium.com

Superplastic formed panels are used for Siemens Desiro train façades as shown in this CAD rendering (image **1**). The aluminium sheet is loaded into the mold (images **2** and **3**). The superplastic forming cycle takes approximately 50 minutes. The demolded part is loaded onto a support structure and CNC trimmed and machined (image **4**). The train front is made in two halves which are brought together in a specially designed jig and tungsten inert gas (TIG) welded (image **5**).

2

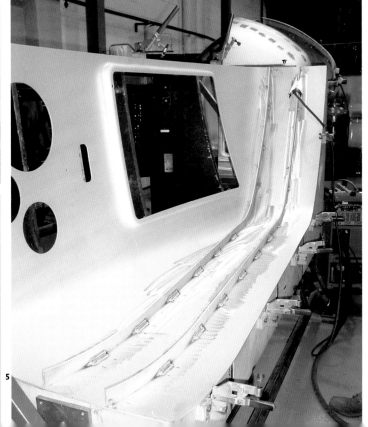

4

5

Ceramic Press Molding

Ceramic press molding is a technique for manufacturing multiple replica ceramic parts with permanent molds. Soft clay is forced at high pressure into a plaster mold, which simultaneously shapes and dries the material. It is used in the production of kitchen and tableware, including pots, cups, bowls, dishes and plates.

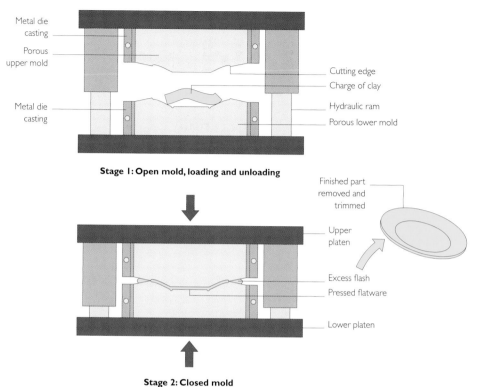

Metal die casting

Porous upper mold

Metal die casting

Cutting edge

Charge of clay

Hydraulic ram

Porous lower mold

Stage 1: Open mold, loading and unloading

Finished part removed and trimmed

Upper platen

Excess flash

Pressed flatware

Lower platen

Stage 2: Closed mold

Essential Information

VISUAL QUALITY	●●●●●●●
SPEED	●●●●●●●
TOOLING COST	●●●●●●●
UNIT COST	●●●●●●●
ENVIRONMENT	●●●●●●●

Related processes include:
• Ram Pressing

Alternative and competing processes include:
• Ceramic Sintering
• Ceramic Slip Casting
• Ceramic Wheel Throwing
• Jiggering and Jolleying

What is Ceramic Press Molding?

This is an automated process that forms parts by hydraulic action. It is also referred to as ram pressing. In stage one, a charge of mixed clay is loaded into the lower mold. In stage two, the upper and lower molds are brought together at high pressure. During the pressing cycle the warm plaster molds draw moisture from the clay, to accelerate the hardening process. The perimeters of each mold cavity on the upper and lower section come together to cut the excess flash from the clay part. The pressing process is rapid and can produce up to six cycles every minute.

QUALITY The high pressure ensures good surface finish, fine reproduction of detail and, most importantly, excellent repeatability. Shrinkage is in the region of 8%, but does depend on the type of material.

TYPICAL APPLICATIONS Uses for press molding ceramics include flatware (such as plates, bowls, cups and saucers, dishes and other kitchen and tableware vessels), sinks and basins, jewelry and tiles.

COST AND SPEED Tooling costs are moderate. Cycle time is around six parts per minute. Labour costs are relatively low. However, manual operations, such as assembly and decoration, increase the costs.

MATERIALS Clay materials, including earthenware, stoneware and porcelain, can be pressed.

ENVIRONMENTAL IMPACTS In all pressing operations scrap is produced at the 'green' stage and so can be directly recycled. There are no harmful by-products from these pottery forming processes. However, the firing process is energy intensive, so therefore the kiln is fully loaded for each firing cycle.

Press-molded tray The moulds can be made to accommodate multiple small parts, or one large part, such as this serving tray. The clay parts are self-supporting and can be demolded immediately.

When compared to ceramic slip casting and throwing, ceramic press molding has the advantage of producing parts that are uniform and compressed and therefore less prone to warpage.

Ceramic press moulding is utilized to make symmetrical shapes as well as oval, square, triangular and irregular ones. Relief profiles and patterns can be applied to the face and underside.

1

Case Study

Ram Pressing Oval Dishes

Featured company Hartley Greens & Co. (Leeds Pottery) www.hartleygreens.com

The two halves of the plaster mold are pre-heated (image **1**). The charges of clay are placed into the lower mold cavity (image **2**) and the two halves are brought together (image **3**). The high pressure forces the clay to flow plastically through the mold cavity and to squeeze out as flash around the edge. The flash is cut as the molds come together and the edges of the mold cavities make contact.

The molds are separated and any excess flash is quickly collected for reprocessing (image **4**). The clay parts are ejected by steam pressure, which is forced through the porous plaster mold (image **5**).

2

3

4

5

Ceramic Slip Casting

Identical hollow shapes with an even wall thickness can be produced with this versatile ceramic production technique. It is used to manufacture high volumes of many familiar household items including tableware and bathroom fittings.

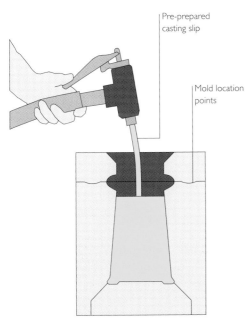

Pre-prepared
casting slip

Mold location
points

Stage 1: Fill with slip

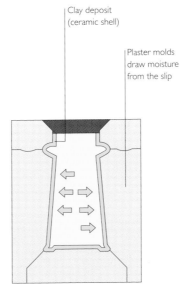

Clay deposit
(ceramic shell)

Plaster molds
draw moisture
from the slip

Stage 2: Ceramic deposit forms

Essential Information

VISUAL QUALITY	●●●●●●○○
SPEED	●●●●○○○○
TOOLING COST	●●●●○○○○
UNIT COST	●●●●○○○○
ENVIRONMENT	●●●●○○○

Alternative and competing processes include:

- Ceramic Press Molding
- Ceramic Sintering
- Ceramic Wheel Throwing
- Jiggering and Jolleying

What is Ceramic Slip Casting?

The casting slip is prepared by mixing together clay, silicate, soda ash and water. In stage one, the mold is filled with the slip and left to stand for five to 25 minutes. The length of time the slip is in the mold and the ambient temperature determine the wall thickness.

In stage two, the plaster mold draws moisture from the slip, causing the clay platelets to pile up around the mold wall and create a ceramic deposit (shell). When the ideal wall thickness is achieved the slip is drained, or poured, from the mold.

Notes for Designers

QUALITY The materials used in slip casting are generally quite brittle and porous, which means that they are not very tough and will fracture under load. Stoneware and porcelain have much better mechanical properties than earthenware.

TYPICAL APPLICATIONS A wide variety of household items such as basins, lighting, vases, teapots, jugs, dishes, bowls, figurines and other utilitarian and decorative objects for the bathroom, kitchen and table.

COST AND SPEED Tooling costs are low. Labour costs are moderate to high due to the level of skill required. This is by far the largest expense and it determines the cost of the parts.

MATERIALS Ceramic materials such as earthenware, terracotta, stoneware and porcelain can all be slip cast.

ENVIRONMENTAL IMPACTS During slip casting there can be up to 15% waste. The majority of this waste can be directly recycled. There are no harmful by-products from these pottery-forming processes. However, the firing process is energy intensive, so therefore the kiln is fully loaded for each firing cycle.

Applying decoration and graphics (above) Decoration, colour and graphics are applied with printed transfers or glaze. Earthenware has to be glazed to be watertight and glazing is used to seal-in colour and decoration on all types of ceramic. Printed transfers are generally only used to apply intricate and precise graphics that would be uneconomical to hand paint, such as the letter 'A' on this children's cup.

Biscuit-fired ceramics (above) Ceramic products made in this way are fired twice. Firstly, they are biscuit fired to remove all the moisture and prepare the ceramic for glazing. Biscuit firing takes place in a kiln over eight hours. The temperature of the parts is raised and then soaked at 1125°C (2057°F) for one hour before cooling slowly.

Large slip-cast bowls (left) This process can be used to produce a range of both simple and complex 3D shapes. Simple shapes can be slip cast in a single operation without any assembly.

Each mold is filled to the brim with earthenware slip (image **1**). The molds are left to stand until a sufficient wall thickness has built up as a deposit on the inside mold wall. The remaining slip is poured from the mold (image **2**).

After demolding, the casting is then left to air-dry before any further work is carried out (image **3**). The outer part is pierced by hand and then all three parts are assembled (image **4**).

After biscuit firing, the glaze is applied and the jug is glaze-fired, which takes up to eight hours. The finished jug is then removed from the kiln watertight and rigid (image **5**). The puzzle jug was designed by Anthony Quinn.

1

2

3

4

5

Steam Bending

Certain woods are suitable for bending over a shaped former when they are steamed and softened. This process, which was industrialized by Michael Thonet during the 1850s, combines industrial techniques with traditional craft. It is used to produce tight and multi-axis bends in solid wood furniture.

Circle bending

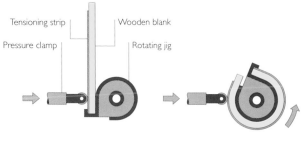

Tensioning strip   Wooden blank

Pressure clamp   Rotating jig

Stage 1: Load   **Stage 2: Bend**

Open bending

Stationary jig
(downward pressure)

Wooden blank

Tensioning
strip

Hydraulic
clamping
system

Stage 1: Load   **Stage 2: Bend**

Essential Information

VISUAL QUALITY	●●●●●●● ○
SPEED	●●●●● ○○○
TOOLING COST	●●●●●● ○○
UNIT COST	●●●●●● ○○
ENVIRONMENT	●●●●●●● ○

Related processes include:
- Circle Bending
- Open Bending

Alternative and competing processes include:
- CNC Machining
- Loom Weaving
- Veneer Laminating

What is Steam Bending?

There are two main types of steam bending: manual operation and power assisted. Manually operated techniques can take many different forms, whereas power-assisted techniques tend to be used for single-axis bends.

Circle bending is designed for forming enclosed rings, such as seat frames and arm rests, whereas open bending is used for open-ended bend profiles such as back rests.

All of the processes work on the same principle: the wooden blank is steamed and softened. In stage one it is clamped in position onto a jig and in stage two it is formed around the jig.

Wood is a natural composite made up of lignin and cellulose. To make the wood adequately pliable the lignin, which bonds the cellulose chains together, must be softened (plasticized) to reduce its strength. This is achieved by thermo-mechanical steam treatment.

Notes for Designers

QUALITY The primary attribute of bentwood is that its grain runs continuously along its entire length. By contrast, a sawn timber profile (CNC machining, page 112) will have had its lengths of grain cut through, thus shortening them and weakening the structure as a whole.

TYPICAL APPLICATIONS Furniture, boats and a range of musical instruments.

COST AND SPEED Tooling costs are low. The cycle time for steam bending is quite slow, due to the length of each stage in the process: soaking (24 hours), steaming (one to three hours) and final drying (24 to 48 hours). Labour costs are moderate to high due to the level of craftsmanship needed.

MATERIALS Beech and ash are common in furniture making; oak is common in construction; elm, ash and willow are traditionally used in boatbuilding; maple is used for musical instruments. Other suitable timbers include birch, hickory, larch, iroko and poplar.

ENVIRONMENTAL IMPACTS Steam bending is a low-impact process. Often timber is locally sourced: for example, Thonet buy all their timber from within a 113 km (70 mile) radius of the processing plant.

Case Study

Steam Bending the Thonet No. 214 Chair

Featured company Thonet www.thonet.de

The classic Thonet No. 214 chair was designed by Michael Thonet in 1859 and was the first mass-produced chair made by the company. There were two versions, with and without arms (image **1**), and to date more of these chairs have been manufactured than any other piece of furniture.

Firstly, the wood is prepared, profiled (image **2**) and then steamed at 104°C (219°F) in a pressure chamber (at 0.6 bars/8.7 psi) for one to three hours (image **3**).

The craftsmen are synchronized in their movements as they clamp the bentwood into the metal jig (image **4**). The part in its jig is loaded into the drying chamber. The parts are removed from the jig after a couple of days (image **5**).

1

2

Thonet A 660 Loop Chair This chair, design by James Irvine for Thonet, is constructed from a continuous loop of bentwood. It is possible to produce almost any shape by seamlessly joining lengths of bentwood together. The only limiting factor is cost.

3

4

5

CNC Machining

CNC machining encompasses a range of shaping processes and is used to manufacture precise and high-quality products. It is used in many industries for shaping metal, plastic, wood, stone, composite and other materials. The process is based on CAD data and so is suitable for both high volumes and one-offs.

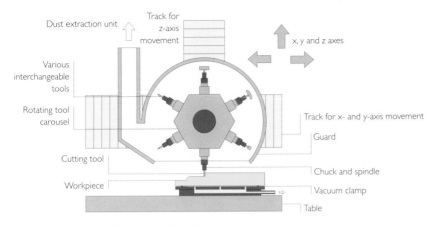

Three-axis **CNC** with tool carousel

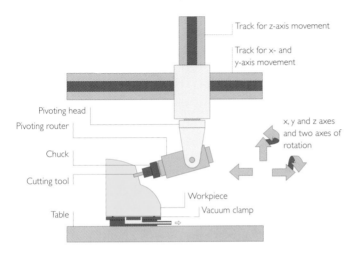

Five-axis **CNC** with interchangeable tools

Essential Information

VISUAL QUALITY	●●●●●●○
SPEED	●●●●●●○
TOOLING COST	●●●●●●●
UNIT	●●●●●●●
ENVIRONMENT	●●●○○○○

Related processes include:
- CNC Lathe Turning
- CNC Milling
- CNC Routing

Alternative and competing processes include:
- CNC Turret Punching
- EDM (Electrical Discharge Machining)
- Laser Cutting
- Rapid Prototyping
- Reaction Injection Molding
- Vacuum Casting
- Veneer Laminating

What is CNC Machining?

Among the many different types of CNC machinery, CNC milling machines and CNC routers are essentially the same. CNC lathes, on the other hand, operate differently because the workpiece is spun rather than the tool. The woodworking and metalworking industries will probably use different names for similar tools and operations – the names and practices can be traced back to when these materials were hand worked using material-specific tools and equipment.

CNC machinery has x- and y-axis tracks (horizontal) and a z-axis track (vertical). Many different tools are used in the cutting process, including cutters (side or face), slot drills (cutting action along the shaft as well as the tip for slotting and profiling), conical, profile, dovetail and flute drills, and ball nose cutters (with a dome head, which is ideal for 3D curved surfaces and hollowing out). By contrast, CNC lathes use single-point cutters because the workpiece is spinning.

Notes for Designers

QUALITY CNC machining produces high-quality parts with close tolerances. Cutting traces can be reduced or eliminated by, for example, sanding, grinding or polishing the part.

TYPICAL APPLICATIONS Almost every factory is now equipped with some form of CNC machinery. It is an essential part of both prototyping and mass-production lines. Applications are therefore diverse and widespread across the manufacturing industry.

COST AND SPEED Tooling costs are minimal and are limited to jigs and other clamping equipment. Cycle time is rapid once the machines are set up.

MATERIALS Almost any material can be CNC machined, including plastic, metal, wood, glass, ceramic and composites.

ENVIRONMENTAL IMPACTS This is a reductive process, so generates waste in operation. Modern CNC systems have very sophisticated dust extraction, which collects all the waste for recycling or incinerating for heat and energy use. Dust that is generated can be hazardous, especially because certain material dusts become volatile when combined.

Steam-bent seat backs The seat backs for the Ercol Windsor are steam bent (page 108) to improve strength and reduce waste.

1

2

3

4

Case Study

CNC Routing the Seat of an Ercol Windsor Chair

Featured company Ercol Furniture www.ercol.com

In this case study, CNC machining is used to make the various beech components that comprise the Ercol Windsor chair (page 117). The combination of techniques is very interesting as it illustrates the vast possibilities of CNC machining working alongside other processes.

Planks of wood are cut to size and loaded onto the CNC machine table (image 1). With a slot drill, the three-axis CNC machine cuts the external profile of the seat (images 2 and 3), a 3D profile. The process takes less than two minutes. The machined seats are stacked up ready for the next operation (image 4).

Case Study

CNC Lathe Turning the Chair Legs

Featured company Ercol Furniture Ltd
www.ercol.com

The legs and spokes for the chair back are rotationally symmetrical and so are produced on a CNC lathe. Cut and profiled timber is loaded automatically into the lathe centres (image **1**). The cutting action is a single, smooth arc made by the cutting head, which carves the workpiece as a continuous shaving (image **2**). These images depict the profiling of a chair leg, which requires a second cutting operation to form a 'bolster' (shoulder) in the top for locating the leg within the seat (image **3**).

The profiled legs are loaded into crates for assembly in batches (image **4**). They still have a 'handle' attached to the top end, which is waste material removed prior to assembly.

1

2

3

4

1

Assembling the Ercol Windsor

Featured company Ercol Furniture www.ercol.com

Each chair is assembled by hand because wood is a 'live' material, which will move and crack and so parts need to be individually inspected. Adhesive is used in all the joints and soaks into the wood grain to create an integral bond between the parts.

Adhesive is added to each joint with a cotton bud (image **1**). The legs and cross bars are then carefully put together and the joints 'hammered home' (images **2** and **3**). The legs come right through the seat and a wedge is driven into the legs' end grain to reinforce the joint.

The finished product is sanded, the legs are cut to length and it is ready for surface treatment (image **4**).

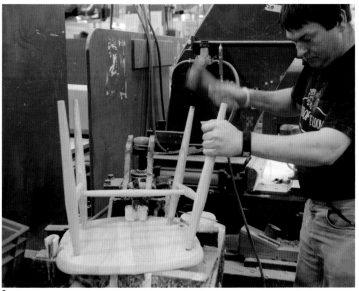

2

3

4

Loom Weaving

Loom weaving is the process of passing strands or strips of material over and under each other to form an intertwined structure. Fibre strength and alignment can be adjusted specifically for each application, reducing weight and material consumption.

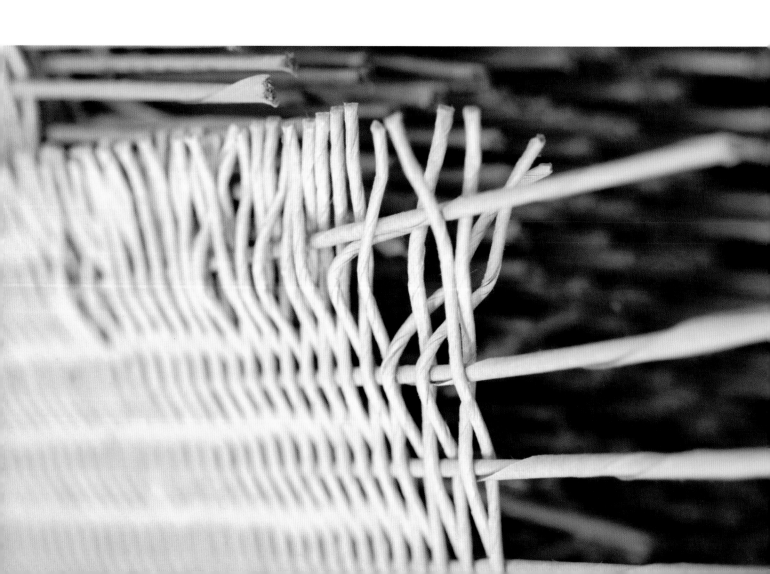

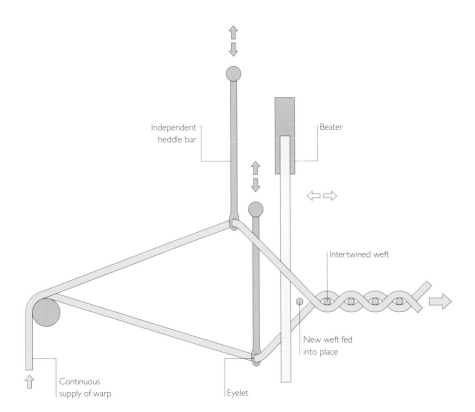

Independent
heddle bar

Beater

Intertwined weft

New weft fed
into place

Continuous
supply of warp

Eyelet

Essential Information

VISUAL QUALITY	●●●●●●●●
SPEED	●●●●●●●●
TOOLING COST	●●●●●●●●
UNIT COST	●●●●●●●●
ENVIRONMENT	●●●●●●●●

Related processes include:
• Loom Caning

Alternative and competing processes include:
• Foam Molding
• Steam Bending
• Upholstery

What is Loom Weaving?

Weaving rigid textiles on a loom consists of three movements repeated many times: raising and lowering the heddle bars, feeding the weft and beating.

Each strand of warp is fed through an eyelet in the heddle bar. The heddle bars are operated individually or as a set, and are computer guided or moved by depressing a foot pedal. Moving them up and down determines whether the warp or weft will be visible from the top side. This is how patterns are made, and they can be very intricate. In the diagram the heddles are separated into two sets, which creates a basket-weave pattern.

A weft is fed into the space between the fibres and in front of the beater. The beater is a series of blunt blades that sit between each fibre. They are used to 'beat' each weft tightly into the overlapping warp.

The weft is held in place by the beater while the lower heddle bar moves up and the upper heddle bar moves down, which locks the weft between the warps. The process is repeated to form the next run.

Notes for Designers

QUALITY The majority of contemporary weaving is carried out on computer-controlled looms, which produce high-quality, repeatable materials.

TYPICAL APPLICATIONS Weaving is used in many different areas of furniture construction. Typical products include stools, chairs, tables, sofas, beds, lights, storage boxes, blinds and screens.

COST AND SPEED There are no tooling costs unless the weave is formed over a mold. Even then the tooling costs tend to be low. Cycle time depends on size, shape and the complexity of the weave or 3D product.

MATERIALS Woven furniture was traditionally handmade using natural fibres such as rattan, willow and bamboo. Mass-production methods can also produce continuous woven materials from metal, paper, plastic and wood.

ENVIRONMENTAL IMPACTS This process creates products with minimal materials. The mechanical join is formed by intertwining materials. Therefore, there are no chemicals, toxins or other hazards associated with melting, fusing, or otherwise altering materials, to join and shape them.

Lloyd Loom Nemo Chair The Lloyd Loom Nemo chair, designed by Studio Dillon in 1998, is made up of a single steam-bent ring, onto which the 3D and self-supporting loom woven material is fixed.

Case Study

Loom Weaving Upholstery

Featured company Lloyd Loom of Spalding
www.lloydloom.com

This case study demonstrates weaving upholstery for a bentwood structure. The example being made is the Lloyd Loom Burghley chair.

The warp is made by twisting strips of Kraft paper into tight fibres. The weft is structural and has a metal filament along its centre.

Each of the looms is loaded with 664 bobbins of twisted paper warp (image **1**). The looms produce flat and continuous woven material 2 m (6.6 ft) wide (image **2**).

The woven material is transferred onto a steam-bent structural framework (image **3**). The edge is stapled with a braid of twisted paper to secure the strands and prevent any fraying (image **4**).

2

3

1

Loom-woven cane The sheets of cane are pre-woven on a loom. There are many different types and patterns, but this octagonal pattern is the most popular. It is a reproduction of the traditional seven-step hand-caning technique known as strand cane.

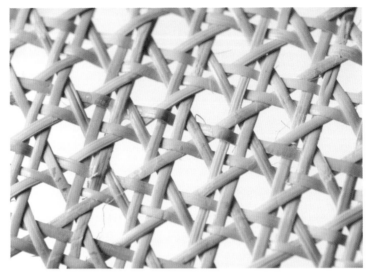

Plain weave Plain weave is the most basic weaving pattern. It is a simple 'one up, one down' pattern. Basketweave is the same pattern, but is made up of bundles of fibres passing under and over one another, rather than a single fibre.

Twill weave Twill, or herringbone, is a diagonal pattern created by overlapping two strands or more at a time.

1

Case Study

Upholstering the Thonet S 32 with Loom-woven Cane

Featured company Thonet www.thonet.de

The S 32 (image **1**) was designed by Marcel Breuer and production at Thonet began in 1929. It is among one of the most mass produced tubular steel chairs in history. First of all the cane is cut into strips and soaked to make it pliable. The cane is then hammered into a groove in the bentwood seat back using a specially shaped tool (image **2**) and a spline of cane is pressed into the groove to secure the weave.

The excess material is trimmed off and the spline finished off (images **3** and **4**). The assembly is placed into a warm press, which applies even pressure and the finished seat backs are stacked ready for assembly onto the tubular metal frame (image **5**).

2

3

4

5

Laser Cutting

This is a high-precision CNC process that can be used to cut, etch, engrave and mark a variety of materials including plastic, metal, timber, veneer, paper and card, synthetic marble, flexible magnet, textile and fleece, rubber and certain types of glass and ceramic.

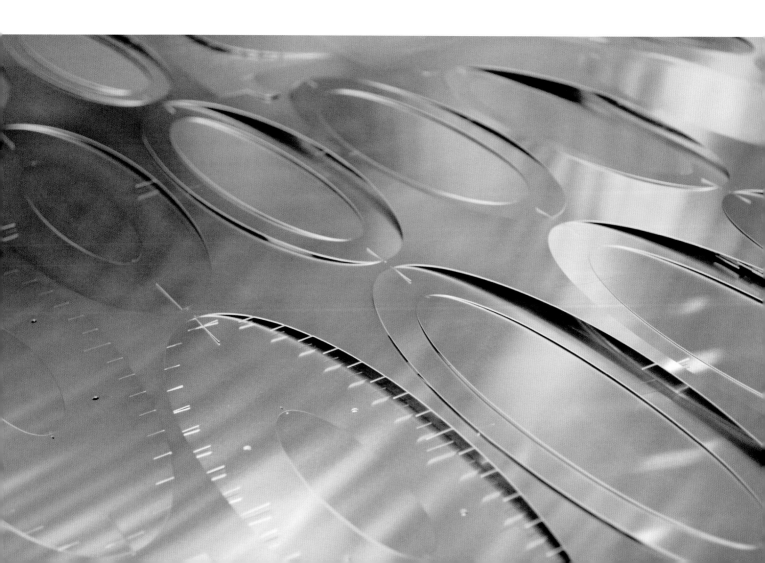

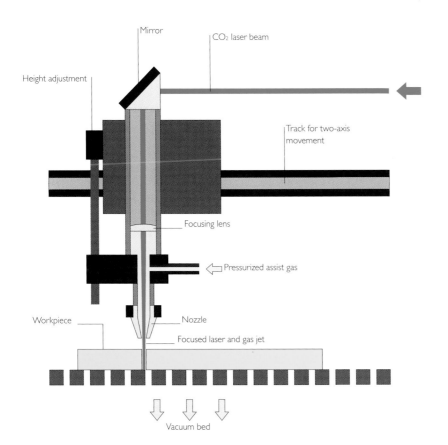

Mirror

CO₂ laser beam

Height adjustment

Track for two-axis movement

Focusing lens

Pressurized assist gas

Workpiece

Nozzle

Focused laser and gas jet

Vacuum bed

Essential Information

VISUAL QUALITY	●●●●●●○○
SPEED	●●●●●○○○
TOOLING COST	●●●●●●○
UNIT COST	●●●●●○○
ENVIRONMENT	●●●●○○○○

Related processes include:
- Laser Engraving
- Laser Scoring

Alternative and competing processes include:
- CNC Engraving
- CNC Machining
- CNC Turret Punching
- EDM (Electrical Discharge Machining)
- Photochemical Machining
- Punching and Blanking
- Water Jet Cutting

What is Laser Cutting?

CO₂ and Nd:YAG laser beams are guided to the cutting nozzle by a series of fixed mirrors. Due to their shorter wavelength, Nd:YAG laser beams can also be guided to the cutting nozzle with flexible fibre-optic cores. This means that they can cut along five axes because the head is free to rotate in any direction.

The laser beam is focused through a lens to a fine spot, between 0.1 mm and 1 mm (0.004–0.04 in.). The high concentration beam melts or vaporizes the material on contact.

Notes for Designers

QUALITY Certain materials, such as thermoplastics, have a very high-quality surface finish when cut in this way. Laser processes produce perpendicular, smooth, clean cuts in most materials.

TYPICAL APPLICATIONS Applications include furniture, consumer electronics, fashion, signs and trophies, and point of sale.

COST AND SPEED There are no tooling costs for this process. Data is transmitted directly from a CAD file to the laser-cutting machine. Cycle time is rapid but dependent on material thickness. Thicker materials take considerably longer to cut.

MATERIALS This process is ideally suited to cutting thin sheet materials down to 0.2 mm (0.0079 in.); it is possible to cut sheets up to 40 mm (1.57 in.), but thicker materials greatly reduce processing speed. Compatible materials include plastic, metal, timber, veneer, paper and card, synthetic marble, flexible magnet, textile and fleece, rubber and certain types of glass and ceramic.

ENVIRONMENTAL IMPACTS Careful planning will ensure minimal waste, but it is impossible to avoid offcuts that are not suitable for reuse.

Case Study

Laser Cutting the Queen Titania

Featured company Luceplan www.luceplan.com

Alberto Meda and Paolo Rizzatto designed the Queen Titania for Luceplan in 2005 (image **1**). It is a modified (1.4 m/4.6 ft long) version of the Titania, which was first manufactured by Luceplan in 1989.

A sheet of aluminium is loaded in the Nd:YAG laser cutter and the cutting sequence begins (image **2**). The cut parts do not have to be de-burred or treated in any other way, which is a major advantage of laser cutting. Each part is removed from the sheet ready for assembly (image **3**).

The light is assembled in two halves, which are joined by riveting (image **4**).

1

2

Laser-cut acrylic Laser cutting produces a polished edge on certain thermoplastics and so eliminates finishing operations.

3

4

Joining Technology

Hot Plate Welding

Hot plate welding is used to form permanent and hermetic joints in extruded and injection molded thermoplastic parts. It is a very simple process: the joint interface is heated until it plasticizes and then pressed together until it solidifies.

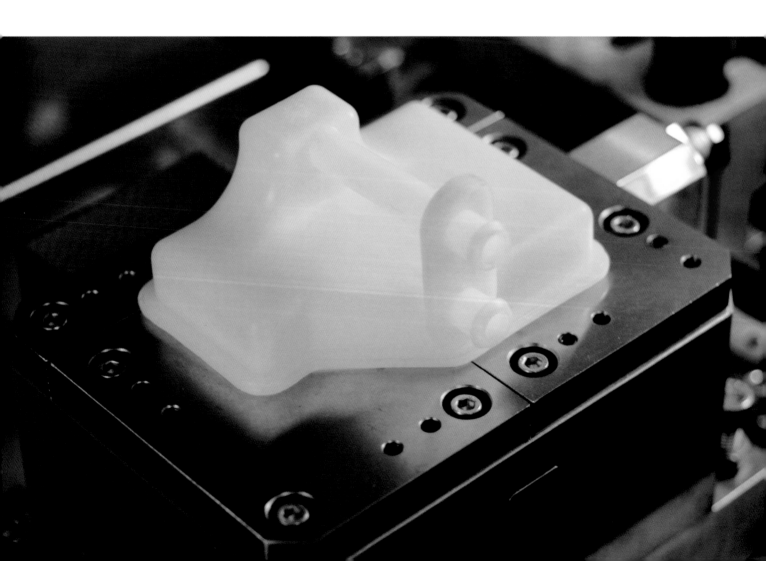

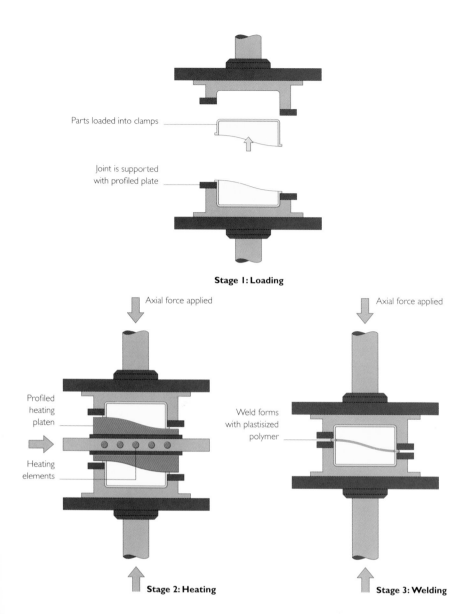

Parts loaded into clamps

Joint is supported with profiled plate

Stage 1: Loading

Axial force applied

Profiled heating platen

Heating elements

Stage 2: Heating

Axial force applied

Weld forms with plastisized polymer

Stage 3: Welding

Essential Information

VISUAL QUALITY   ●●●●●○○○

SPEED   ●●●●●●○○

TOOLING COST   ●●●●○○○○

UNIT COST   ●●●●●○○○

ENVIRONMENT   ●●○○○○○○

Related processes include:
• Platen Welding
• Seam Welding

Alternative and competing processes include:
• Assembly
• Friction Welding
• Staking
• Ultrasonic Welding
• Vibration Welding

What is Hot Plate Welding?

In stage one, the parts are loaded into the tools and are held in place by a small vacuum.

In stage two, the parts are brought into contact with a pre-heated platen, which raises the temperature of the joint interface and plasticizes the outer layers of material.

In stage three, the parts separate from the heated platen, which is withdrawn to allow the parts to be brought together. Pressure is applied and the plasticized joint interfaces mix to form a homogeneous bond.

Notes for Designers

QUALITY The strength of the weld is affected by the design of the part and the type of material. Heating and plasticizing is localized, up to 1 mm (0.04 in.) on either side, and so the process does not affect the structure of the workpiece.

TYPICAL APPLICATIONS The automotive industry is the largest user of hot plate welding. The process is also used for some packaging and pharmaceutical products.

COST AND SPEED Tooling costs are moderately expensive. Cycle time is generally rapid: around 30 seconds. However, complex and large welds can take considerably longer: up to 10 minutes.

MATERIALS Most thermoplastics can be joined in this way, although it is limited to injection molded and extruded parts.

ENVIRONMENTAL IMPACTS This process does not add any material to the joint and there is no waste produced during welding. Hot plate welding has a low environmental impact.

Case Study

Hot Plate Welding an Automotive Part

Featured company Branson Ultrasonics
www.branson-plasticsjoin.com

The part is made of two injection molded halves (image **1**). The top and bottom half are loaded into their respective jigs and are held in place by a small vacuum (image **2**).

Heating takes place on a heated platen (image **3**), which raises the temperature of the material to more than 50°C (122°F) higher than its melting point. After only a few seconds, the tools separate and the heating platen is withdrawn. The parts are then brought together and held under pressure until the joint interface has mixed and solidified. The whole process takes no more than 25 seconds.

The part is removed and checked (image **4**).

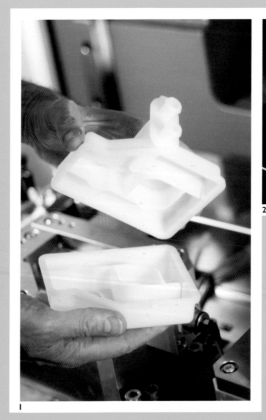

Joint detail showing flash Flash produced by pressure in the welding operation is often left untrimmed. However, it is possible to conceal the joint flash with a flange around the weld area.

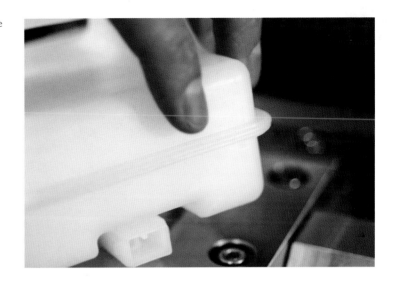

3

4

Ultrasonic Welding

This process forms permanent joints using ultrasonic waves in the form of high-energy vibration. It is the least expensive and fastest plastic welding process – the conversion of electrical energy into mechanical vibration is an efficient use of energy – and so is the first to be considered in many welding applications.

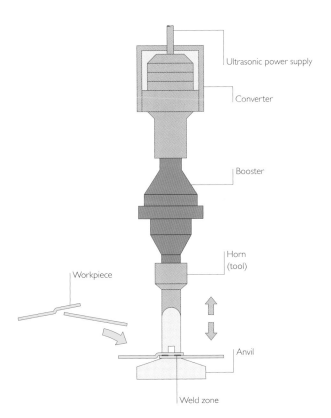

Ultrasonic power supply

Converter

Booster

Horn (tool)

Workpiece

Anvil

Weld zone

Essential Information

VISUAL QUALITY	●●●●●●○○
SPEED	●●●●●●●○
TOOLING COST	●●●○○○○○
UNIT COST	●●●●○○○○
ENVIRONMENT	●●●○○○○○

Related processes include:
• Seam Welding
• Spot Welding

Alternative and competing processes include:
• Assembly
• Friction Welding
• Hot Plate Welding
• Staking
• Vibration Welding

What is Ultrasonic Welding?

Ultrasonic welding works on the principle that electrical energy can be converted into high-energy vibration by means of piezoelectric discs. The crystals that make up the discs expand and contract when electrically charged. In doing so, they convert electrical energy into mechanical energy with 95% efficiency.

The mechanical energy is transferred to the booster, which modifies the amplitude into vibrations suitable for welding. The horn transfers the vibrations to the workpiece. The size and length of the horn are limited because it has to resonate correctly.

Frictional heat is generated at the joint interface which causes the material to plasticize. Pressure is applied which encourages a strong, homogeneous bond to form.

Notes for Designers

QUALITY Ultrasonic welding produces homogeneous bonds between plastic parts. Joint strength is high and hermetic seals are possible.

TYPICAL APPLICATIONS Applications are widespread and include consumer electronics, packaging, safety equipment and nappies.

COST AND SPEED Horns have to be made from high-grade aerospace aluminium or titanium. Even so, tooling costs are generally low. Welding time is typically less than one second.

MATERIALS All thermoplastics can be joined in this way. Textiles and non-woven materials, including thermoplastic fabrics, composite materials, coated paper and mixed fabrics, can be joined, as well as some metals.

ENVIRONMENTAL IMPACTS Ultrasonic welding is an efficient use of energy; almost all of the electrical energy is converted into vibrations at the joint interface, so there is very little heat radiation.

Ultrasonic welding the TSM 6 mobile phone The TSM 6 mobile phone was designed by Product Partners. Ultrasonic welding has been used on the front assembly to produce many different combinations of colour and finish economically.

This process gives greater design freedom because parts that cannot be molded in a single operation can be ultrasonically joined to produce complex, intricate and otherwise impossible geometries.

Boosters are anodized aluminium and coloured to indicate the frequency at which they operate (image **1**).

The parts that are going to be joined (image **2**) make up a small impellor. There is a small step on the blades of the impellor which provides the interference for the shear joint.

The horn is brought into contact with the part and the welding process is completed in less than a second (image **3**). The finished part is removed from the anvil with a permanent hermetic joint (image **4**).

Vibration Welding

Vibration welding is based on friction welding principles. The parts are rubbed together to generate frictional heat, which plasticizes the joint interface. The process is carried out as linear or orbital vibration welding and is used to create homogeneous bonds in plastic parts.

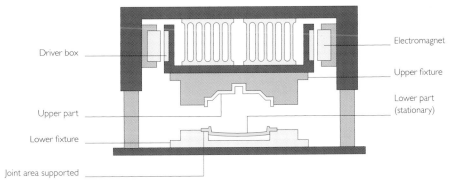

Driver box

Upper part

Lower fixture

Joint area supported

Electromagnet

Upper fixture

Lower part
(stationary)

Stage 1: Loaded mold during linear vibration welding

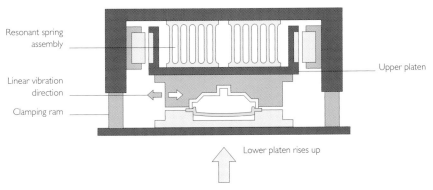

Resonant spring
assembly

Linear vibration
direction

Clamping ram

Upper platen

Lower platen rises up

Stage 2: Closed mold, welding and clamping

What is Vibration Welding?

The two techniques for vibration welding, linear and orbital, are based on the same principle. In stage one, one part is placed in the lower platen and the part to which it is to be joined is positioned in the upper platen. In stage two, the heat necessary to melt the plastic is generated by pressing the parts together and vibrating them.

Heat generated by the resulting friction melts the plastic at the interface within two to three seconds. Vibration motion is then stopped and pressure is maintained until the plastic solidifies to form a strong bond.

Notes for Designers

QUALITY It is possible to form strong hermetic seals. Homogeneous bonds can be achieved in certain materials.

TYPICAL APPLICATIONS Although this process is typically utilized in the automotive industry, it is now steadily becoming more widespread in, for example, medical, consumer electronics and white-good appliances.

COST AND SPEED Tooling has to be designed and built specifically for each part. Cycle time is rapid.

MATERIALS Thermoplastics are suitable for this process, and some polymer-based composite materials, thermoplastic films and fabrics can also be welded in this way.

ENVIRONMENTAL IMPACTS There are no materials added to the joint to form the weld, which means that this process does not generate any waste.

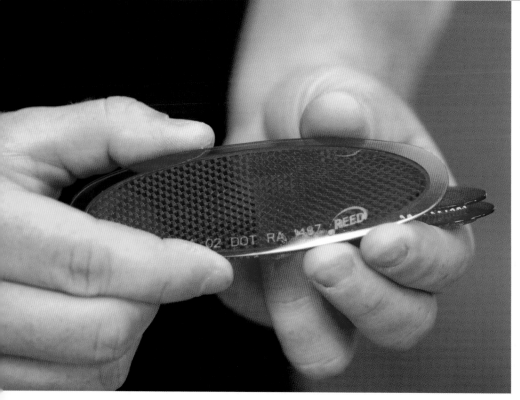

Vibration welding part design Vibration welding is most suitable for injection molded and extruded parts. However, two essential requirements must be taken into account when considering the process. Firstly, the design must allow for the required movement between the parts to generate sufficient frictional heat; the plane of vibration must be flat, or at least within 10°. Secondly, the parts must be designed so that they can be gripped adequately to ensure sufficient energy transmission to the joint.

1

2

3

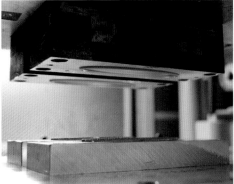

4

Case Study

Vibration Welding an Automotive Sidelight

Featured company Branson Ultrasonics
www.branson-plasticsjoin.com

A pair of right- and left-hand sidelights is being molded simultaneously. The red reflectors (image **1**) are placed into the lower platen, then the sidelight housings (image **2**) are positioned into the upper platen, where they are held by a vacuum (image **3**).

During the welding cycle the lower platen holding the stationary part (in this case the red reflectors) rises to meet the upper platen (image **4**), forcing the parts together at high pressure.

The welding process lasts no more than two to 15 seconds. The parts are released from the clamps. They are quality checked (image **5**) and packed for shipping.

5

Staking

These are clean and efficient processes used to assemble injection molded thermoplastic parts with other materials by heating and deforming plastic studs into permanent joints. There are two main techniques: hot air and ultrasonic staking.

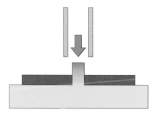

Stage 1: Applying hot air

Stage 2: Applying cold stake

Essential Information

VISUAL QUALITY	●●●●○○○
SPEED	●●●●●○
TOOLING COST	●●●●●●
UNIT COST	●●●●○○○
ENVIRONMENT	●●●○○○○

Related processes include:
- Hot Air Staking
- Ultrasonic Staking

Alternative and competing processes include:
- Assembly
- Friction Welding
- Hot Plate Welding
- Ultrasonic Welding
- Vibration Welding

What is Hot Air Staking?

Hot air staking is a two-stage process. In stage one, hot air is directed at the stud. The temperature of the air is determined by the plasticizing point of the material. In stage two, a cold stake with a profiled head presses down onto the hot stud. This simultaneously forms and cools the stud and joins the materials.

Round studs are typically 0.5 mm to 5 mm (0.02–0.2 in.) in diameter. Rectangular and hollow studs can be much larger, as long as the wall thickness is thin enough for staking.

Notes for Designers

QUALITY These are permanent joints. The strength of the joint is determined by the diameter of the stud and mechanical properties of the parent material.

TYPICAL APPLICATIONS Applications in the automotive industry include control panels, dashboards and door linings. Staking is ideal for joining electrical components into plastic housings because the studs are insulating.

COST AND SPEED Tooling costs are low and cycle time is rapid. Ultrasonic staking can form joints in 0.5 to two seconds. Hot air staking cycle times are five to 15 seconds.

MATERIALS This process is limited to injection molded, thermoplastic parts.

ENVIRONMENTAL IMPACTS Staking eliminates consumables such as rivets, screws and clips.

Multiple fixing points Multiple studs can be heated and formed simultaneously to form large joint areas. It is possible to produce watertight seals by sandwiching a rubber seal in the assembly.

There are no restrictions on the layout, pattern or number of studs. Pressure is applied during operation and so the joints are tight and free from vibration.

Case Study

Hot Air Staking a Lamp Housing

Featured company Branson Ultrasonics
www.branson-plasticsjoin.com

This case study demonstrates a typical hot air staking application. The parts being assembled are the lamp housing and electrical contacts.

The lamp housing is placed into a tool and the pressed metal contacts are placed over the studs (images **1** and **2**).

A stream of hot air is directed at each stud for a few seconds. Cold dome-headed tools form the hot plastic studs (image **3**). The stakes retract and the assembly operation is complete (image **4**).

1

2

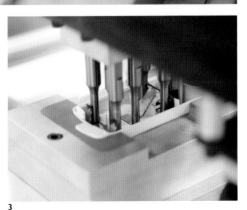

3

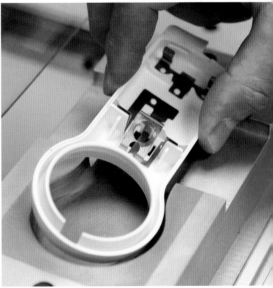

4

What is Ultrasonic Staking?

Round studs are typically 0.5 mm to 5 mm (0.02–0.2 in.). Rectangular and hollow studs can be much larger, as long as the wall thickness is thin enough for staking.

Ultrasonic staking is more rapid than hot air techniques and only takes a few seconds. It is a single-stage operation in which the stud is heated up by ultrasonic vibrations. As the stud is heated up it softens and is formed by pressure applied by the tool.

Ultrasonic welding is suitable for a range of other operations including welding, sealing and cutting.

Stage 1: Assembly

Stage 2: Ultrasonic staking

Ultrasonic horns (tools) for staking It is possible to form dome, knurled, split and other profiles into the top of the stud when staking. The shape of the tool is adjusted to fit the requirements of the application and stud diameter.

1

Case Study

Ultrasonic Staking

Featured company Branson Ultrasonics
www.branson-plasticsjoin.com

In this case, ultrasonic staking is used to
join a rubber seal onto an injection molded
part. The two parts are assembled on
a jig (image **1**). The studs are rectangular
to provide a larger joint area.

The ultrasonic horns are mounted onto
a single booster and work simultaneously.
The inside of the horn forms the stud into
the desired shape.

The ultrasonic horns compress onto the
parts and apply vibrations to heat up the
studs (image **2**). The ultrasonic vibrations
form the studs very quickly. After a couple
of seconds the joint is complete and the
horns retract (image **3**).

2

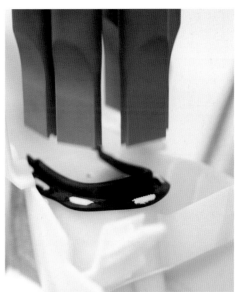

3

CNC Joinery

There are many joint profiles that are suitable for CNC machining, including mitre, housing and dovetail. A combination of cabinetmaking skills, modern sheet materials and CNC operations are utilized in the production of one-offs as well as high volumes of identical parts.

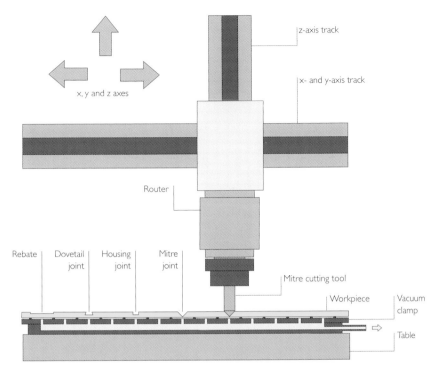

z-axis track

x- and y-axis track

x, y and z axes

Router

Rebate | Dovetail joint | Housing joint | Mitre joint

Mitre cutting tool

Workpiece

Vacuum clamp

Table

What is CNC Machining?

CNC joinery is typically produced using a router that moves along three axes, whereby x and y are horizontal and z is vertical. For non-vertical operations, such as drilling a hole at an angle of 45°, a five-axis CNC machine, which is capable of travelling and rotating around all three axes, is required (see page 113).

In operation, the sheet material is held on the table by a vacuum clamp which eliminates the need for mechanical clamps. The top and bottom side of the sheet are machined separately.

Machine tools are produced in a wide range of standard and bespoke profiles that are capable of producing mitre, housing, dovetail and other rebated profiles. The type of joint depends on the material and application.

Joints and profiles are cut simultaneously, reducing the number of operations required.

Notes for Designers

QUALITY CNC machined joint profiles are accurate to within microns, although this depends on the quality and hardness of the raw material. Cutting traces can be reduced or eliminated by, for example, sanding, grinding or polishing the part.

TYPICAL APPLICATIONS Almost every factory is now equipped with some form of CNC machinery. It is an essential part of both prototyping and mass-production lines. Therefore, applications are diverse and widespread across the manufacturing industry.

COST AND SPEED Tooling costs are minimal and are limited to jigs and other clamping equipment. Cycle time is rapid once the machines are set up. Labour costs depend largely on the complexity of assembly operations.

MATERIALS Almost any material can be CNC machined, including plastic, metal, wood, glass, ceramic and composites.

ENVIRONMENTAL IMPACTS This is a reductive process, so generates waste in operation. Modern CNC systems have very sophisticated dust extraction, which collects all the waste for recycling or incinerating for heat and energy use. Dust that is generated can be hazardous, especially because certain material dusts become volatile when combined.

Case Study

CNC Machining Rega Speaker Cabinets

Featured company ProCut Ltd www.procutuk.co.uk and Rega Research www.rega.co.uk

The acoustic properties of the wood combined with the speaker driver units have been calculated for optimal performance. Therefore, it is essential that the geometry of the speaker cabinets is precise and each unit is identical. CNC joinery is ideal for this application.

A range of CNC operations are carried out on the raw material including cutting windows with rebates to house the

1

speaker driver units (image **1**), housing joints for internal divisions, lap joints and mitre joints (image **2**).

The process is rapid and precise. Once machining is complete adhesive is applied to the joints and the front, back and sides are assembled simultaneously (image **3**).

Once the adhesive has cured sufficiently the Cherry veneer cabinets are varnished and the speaker driver units installed (image **4**). Finally, the pair are tested to confirm their acoustic properties are accurate (image **5**).

2

3

4

5

Assembly

Multiple-part products require assembly. A wide range of joining techniques, including thermal, mechanical and adhesive bonding processes, are utilized to join dissimilar materials. Recent environmental initiatives have resulted in the development of improved temporary fixing techniques that enable design for disassembly.

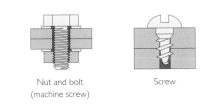

Nut and bolt
(machine screw)

Screw

Threaded fasteners

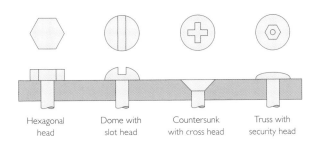

Hexagonal
head

Dome with
slot head

Countersunk
with cross head

Truss with
security head

Screw head profiles

Essential Information

VISUAL QUALITY	●●●●●●○○
SPEED	●●●○○○○○
TOOLING COST	●●○○○○○○
UNIT COST	●●●●●○○○
ENVIRONMENT	●●○○○○○○

Related processes include:
• Adhesive Bonding
• Mechanical Fasteners
• Riveting
• Soldering and Brazing
• Spot Welding

Alternative and competing processes include:
• Arc Welding
• Friction Welding
• Hot Plate Welding
• Power Beam Welding

What is Mechanical Assembly?

Mechanical fixings are designed into parts wherever possible to avoid adding unnecessary materials and operations. For example, injection molded parts can be designed with snap fits and over-molded threaded fasteners (page 38).

If this is not practical or feasible additional assembly operations are undertaken. These include thermal, mechanical and adhesive bonding processes. Typically, a combination of many different assembly processes is utilized for complex products and those consisting of multiple materials.

Mechanical fasteners include rivets, threaded and sprung clips. Threaded fasteners are very common due to their versatility. The main types are bolts (small diameter bolts are also referred to as machine screws) and screws. Bolts have a cylindrical shaft and helix thread. They are held in place by threading into a nut or threaded hole (known as tapped).

There are many hundreds of types of screws including wood, self-tapping, thread rolling, drywall, dowel and so on. The type of screw depends on the materials and application.

Notes for Designers

QUALITY Joints are inevitable in all but the simplest products and so assembly procedures have to be considered in the design and engineering of products. Careful planning reduces quality issues such as joint alignment, location and visibility. The operator is an essential consideration in the design process.

TYPICAL APPLICATIONS Applications cover almost every industry sector including automotive, consumer electronics and furniture.

COST AND SPEED Tooling costs are minimal and are limited to jigs and other clamping equipment. Cycle time is rapid once the machines are set up. Labour costs depend on the complexity of the product.

MATERIALS All types of materials can be joined. The selected materials and required tolerances will determine the assembly procedures and subsequent design details.

ENVIRONMENTAL IMPACTS Assembly with temporary fixings can reduce the environmental impact of a product because it can be dismantled at the end of its useful life for recycling. However, this is not always practical or feasible and so ideally parts are designed in a single material with integrated assembly features such as snap fits.

Case Study

Assembling a Rega Speaker Driver Unit

Featured company Rega Research www.rega.co.uk

The speaker driver is an ideal case study because there are many different materials and assembly techniques utilized in the production. This case study demonstrates adhesive, thermal and mechanical assembly operations.

The metal base (which will be magnetized) and frame (image **1**) are joined together using adhesive bonding and mechanical fasteners. This combination reduces potential vibration. The adhesive is put in place and the two parts are joined together with self-tapping screws (image **2**). As the screws are driven into pre-holes they cut their own thread. This technique reduces costly thread-tapping operations.

A bead of cyanacrylate adhesive, which is the same as 'super glue', is applied to the top and bottom contact points between the frame and the cone (image **3**). The cone is precisely located and an activator is sprayed onto the adhesive to accelerate the curing process (image **4**).

Finally, the input wires are located (image **5**) and soldered in place. The soft metal filler is drawn into the joint by capillary action and the heat of the soldering iron (image **6**).

The finished speaker driver unit is now ready to be assembled into the speaker cabinet (image **7**) (page 150).

Upholstery

Upholstery is a highly skilled manual process and the quality of the craftsmanship sets furniture apart. It is the process of bringing together the hard and soft components of a piece of furniture to form the finished article. The same techniques are used for low volumes and mass production.

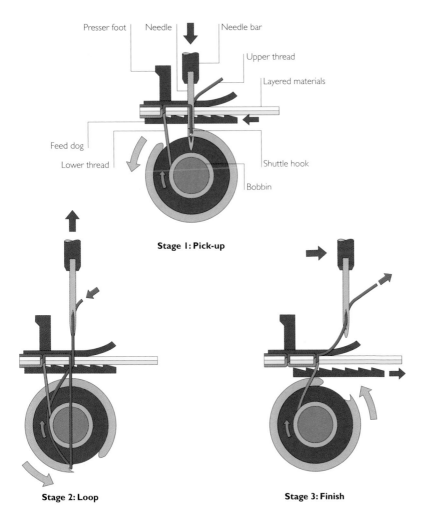

Presser foot   Needle   Needle bar

Upper thread

Layered materials

Feed dog

Lower thread

Shuttle hook

Bobbin

Stage 1: Pick-up

Stage 2: Loop

Stage 3: Finish

Essential Information

VISUAL QUALITY	●●●●●●●○
SPEED	●●●●●●○○
TOOLING COST	●●●●●●○○
UNIT COST	●●●●●●○
ENVIRONMENT	●●●●●○○

Related processes include:
• Machine Lockstitching

Alternative and competing processes include:
• Foam Molding
• Loom Weaving
• Steam Bending

What is Machine Lockstitching?

Lockstitching is a mechanized process. The needle and shuttle hook are synchronized by a series of gears and shafts powered by an electric motor. In stage one, the upper thread is carried through the textile by the needle, and the lower thread is wound on a bobbin. The needle pierces the layers of material and stops momentarily. In stage two, a spinning shuttle hook picks up the upper thread. The shuttle hook loops behind the lower thread which is held under tension on the bobbin. In stage three, as the shuttle continues to rotate, tension is applied to the upper thread, which pulls it tight to form the next stitch. Meanwhile, the feed dog progresses forward, catches the fabric and pulls it into place for the next drop of the needle. The fabric is supported between the presser foot and feed dog. Industrial sewing machines can repeat this sequence over 5,000 times every minute.

QUALITY The visual quality is largely dependent on the skill of the upholsterer and the quality of the fabrics, while the comfort is affected by the quality of the foam padding.

TYPICAL APPLICATIONS Upholstery is used extensively in furniture and interior design and to make 'soft' furnishings for automotive, marine, transport and office environments.

COST AND SPEED There are no tooling costs, but jigs may be required. Overall cycle time is reasonably long due to the number of operations and their complexity. Labour costs are relatively high.

MATERIALS Any fabric can be used for upholstery. The area of applications, such as home, office or automotive, determines the most suitable types. Fabrics with a high resistance to wear include polyamide (PA) nylon, polyester, thermoplastic polyurethane (TPU), polyvinyl chloride (PVC) and polypropylene (PP). Other suitable materials include leather, flock, raffia, mohair, cotton and canvas.

ENVIRONMENTAL IMPACTS Upholstery is the culmination of many different processes and as a consequence a typical sofa will include many different materials that have varying environmental implications.

Eye Chair The Eye Chair was designed by Jackie Choi for Boss Design and production began in 2005. The cushion is molded polyurethane foam (page 54). It has a metal structure for support and plastic or wooden panels to which the covering materials can be fixed. It is upholstered in either fabric or leather.

1

2

3

4

5

6

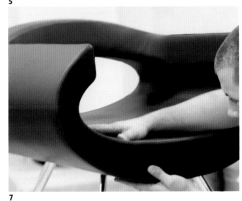

7

Case Study

Upholstering the Boss Eye Chair

Featured company Boss Design
www.boss-design.co.uk

The leather is prepared by a pattern cutter (image **1**), who works out the least wasteful arrangement of patterns on the sheet. If possible, the patterns are cut from a single skin and stitched together (image **2**).

The foam is covered in soft polyester or down lining, which helps smooth over imperfections (image **3**). Then the cover is fitted, covered with adhesive and pulled over the foam (image **4**). The adhesive is not sticky at this point.

A separately upholstered panel snap fits onto the over-molded plastic panel to conceal the trimmed edges (image **5**).

The leather cover is now securely in place. However, there are undercuts to which the cover must be bonded if it is to retain its shape. This is done with steam and a soft cloth (image **6**). The heat from the steam softens and activates the adhesive, so that as the cover is gently pushed into the desired shape, the adhesive bonds to the foam. The chair is inspected prior to packing and shipping (image **7**).

Finishing Technology

Tampo Printing

Tampo printing, also known as pad printing, is used to print on surfaces that are flat, concave, convex or even all three. This is possible because the ink is applied to the product using a flexible silicone pad that wraps around the surface of the part without loss of shape or quality.

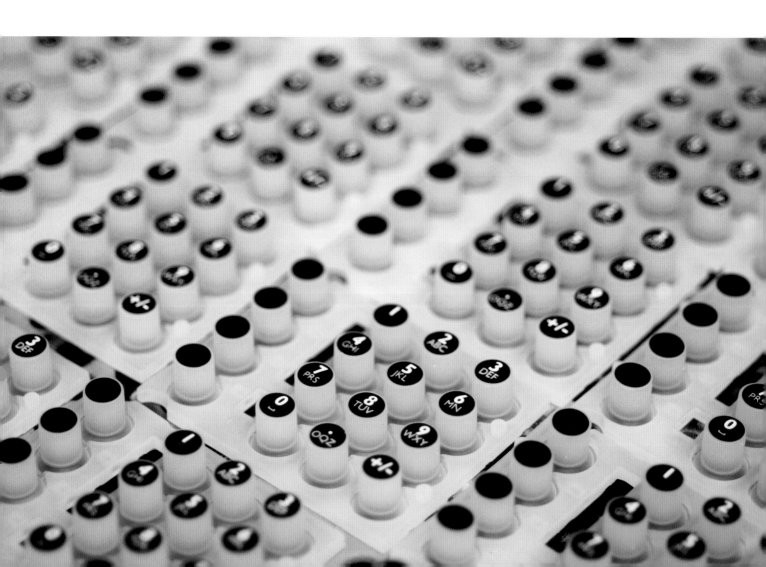

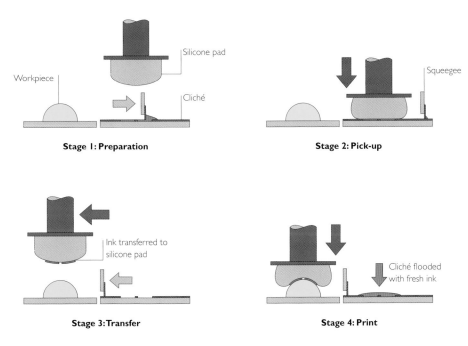

Stage 1: Preparation

Stage 2: Pick-up

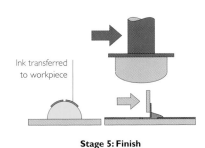

Stage 3: Transfer

Stage 4: Print

Stage 5: Finish

Essential Information

VISUAL QUALITY	◐◐◐◐◐◐◐
SPEED	◐◐◐◐◐◐◐
TOOLING COST	◐◐◐◐◐◐◐
UNIT COST	◐◐◐◐◐◐◐
ENVIRONMENT	◐◐◐◐◐◐◐

Alternative and competing processes include:
- Foil Blocking
- Hydro-transfer Printing
- Screen Printing

What is Tampo Printing?

In stage one, the cliché is flooded with ink. The engraved design in the cliché is very shallow and the thickness of the finished print. In stage two, the silicone pad picks up the ink from the cliché.

In stage three, the silicone pad moves over to the product. Meanwhile, the squeegee tracks back across the cliché, which is about to be flooded with ink again.

In stage four, the silicone pad is compressed onto the workpiece. It wraps around the surface profile and the ink is transferred to the surface.

In stage five, the part is finished and the silicone pad tracks back to the cliché where a fresh charge of ink has been flooded and wiped clean.

Notes for Designers

QUALITY The definition of detail is determined by the design of the cliché and can incorporate details 0.1 mm (0.004 in.) thin spaced 0.1 mm (0.004 in.) apart. The smooth silicone will transfer all of the ink it picks up onto the surface of the part.

TYPICAL APPLICATIONS Applications include keypads on handheld devises, remote controls and mobile phones. Tampo printing is widely used to mark consumer electronics and sports equipment with logos, instructions and images.

COST AND SPEED Tooling costs are low. The cliché is typically the most expensive but is limited to 100 mm × 100 mm (3.94 in.). Cycle time is rapid. Inks can be laid down wet-on-wet, which is an advantage for multiple-colour printing. Labour costs are minimal.

MATERIALS Almost all materials can be printed in this way. Some plastic materials will require surface pre-treatment to ensure high print quality.

ENVIRONMENTAL IMPACTS This process is limited to solvent-based inks and associated thinners that may contain harmful chemicals.

Case Study

Tampo Printing a Backlit Keypad

Featured company Rubbertech2000
www.rubbertech2000.co.uk

In this case, tampo printing is being used to apply the negative graphics. The buttons have already been printed white and yellow. These are the colours that will be seen when it is illuminated. The silicone pad is brought into alignment with the cliché (image **1**) and pressed down lightly to pick up the ink (image **2**). The ink on the silicone pad is a thin film (image **3**). The silicone pad aligns with the part and is pressed onto it (image **4**). Pressure is applied and the ink is transferred onto the surface of the workpiece (image **5**).

On the finished part (image **6**), the black masks the light so that coloured numbers are displayed when backlit.

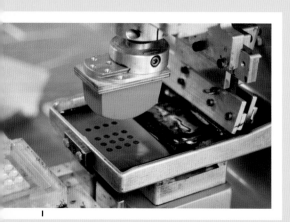

1

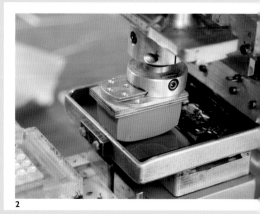

2

3

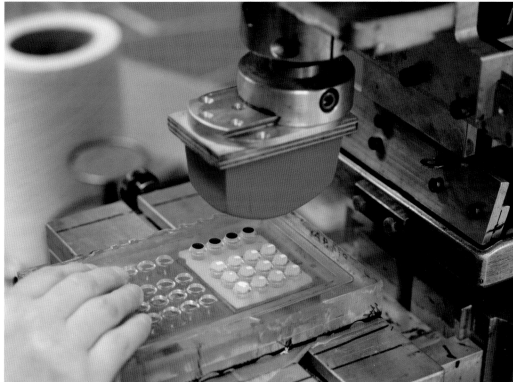

4

5

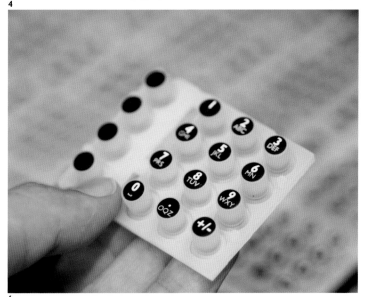

6

Screen Printing

This versatile printing process is used to apply accurate and registered coatings to a range of substrates including textiles, paper, glass, ceramic, plastic and metal. Most types of ink are suitable, which means this method can print graphics onto almost any flat or cylindrical surface.

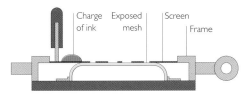

Charge | Exposed | Screen
of ink | mesh | Frame

Stage 1: Load

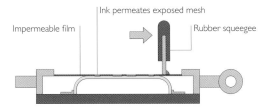

Ink permeates exposed mesh

Impermeable film | Rubber squeegee

Stage 2: Screen print

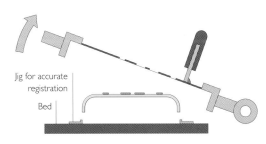

Jig for accurate
registration

Bed

Stage 3: Unload

Essential Information

VISUAL QUALITY	●●●●●●○
SPEED	●●●●●●○
TOOLING COST	●●●●●●○
UNIT COST	●●●●●●○
ENVIRONMENT	●●●●●●○

Related processes include:
• Window Printing

Alternative and competing processes include:
• Foil Blocking
• Hydro-transfer Printing
• Tampo Printing

What is Screen Printing?

This is a wet printing process. A charge of ink is deposited onto the screen, and a rubber squeegee is used to spread the ink evenly across the screen. Those areas protected by the impermeable film (stencil) are not printed.

The screens are made up of a frame, over which a light mesh is stretched. The mesh is typically made up of nylon, polyester or stainless steel. Each colour requires a separate screen.

There are four main types of ink: water-based, solvent-based, polyvinyl chloride- (PVC-) based plastisol and UV curing.

Water and solvent-based inks are air-dried or heated to accelerate the process. PVC-based plastisol inks are used mainly to print textiles. They have varying levels of flexibility, determined by the quantity of plastisol. UV inks contain chemical initiators which cause polymerization when exposed to UV light. These inks have superior colour and clarity, but are also the most expensive.

QUALITY Screen printing produces graphics with clean edges. The definition of detail and thickness of printed ink is determined by the size of mesh used in the screen. Heavier gauges will deposit more ink, but have lower resolution of detail.

TYPICAL APPLICATIONS Ink can be screen printed directly onto a product's surface, or onto an adhesive label that is bonded to the surface. Mass-production applications are widespread and include packaging, consumer electronics, banknotes and clothes.

COST AND SPEED Tooling costs are low, but depend on the number of colours. Mechanized production methods are the most rapid, and can print up to 30 parts per minute. The labour costs can be high for manual techniques. Mechanized systems can run for long periods without intervention.

MATERIALS Almost any material can be screen printed, including paper, plastic, rubber, metal, ceramic and glass.

ENVIRONMENTAL IMPACTS PVC-, formaldehyde- and solvent-based inks contain harmful chemicals, but they can be reclaimed and recycled to avoid water contamination. Screens are recycled by dissolving the impermeable film away from the mesh so that it can be reused.

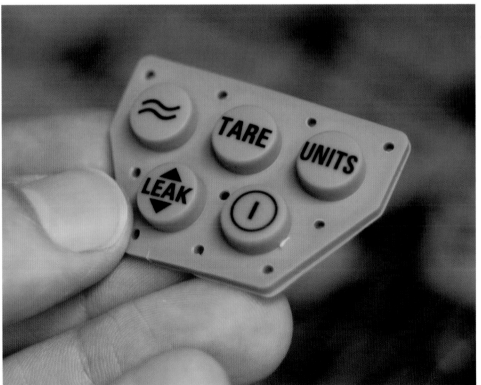

Screen-printed plastic (above) There is a vast range of colours, including Pantone and RAL ranges. Equally, there are numerous types of ink such as clear varnish, metallic, pearlescent, fluorescent, thermochromatic and foam.

Screen-printed rubber keypad (right) Screen printing reproduces fine details well: such as on the buttons of this compression molded (page 14) rubber keypad.

The parts are checked and loaded onto a conveyor belt (image **1**). An operator collects each part and places it into the screen-printing jig (image **2**). A rubber squeegee is used to spread the ink across the surface of the screen (image **3**). Pressure is applied during spreading to ensure that the ink penetrates the permeable areas of mesh and builds up a dense layer of colour with clean edges.

For optimum results, the parts are placed back onto the conveyor belt and the drying process is accelerated in an oven. The finished parts are inspected and packed (image **4**).

1

2

3

4

Anodizing

The surface of aluminium, magnesium and titanium can be anodized to form a protective oxide layer. Aluminium anodizing is naturally light grey, but can be electrolytically coloured, or dyed, with a range of vivid colours including red, green, blue, gold, bronze and black.

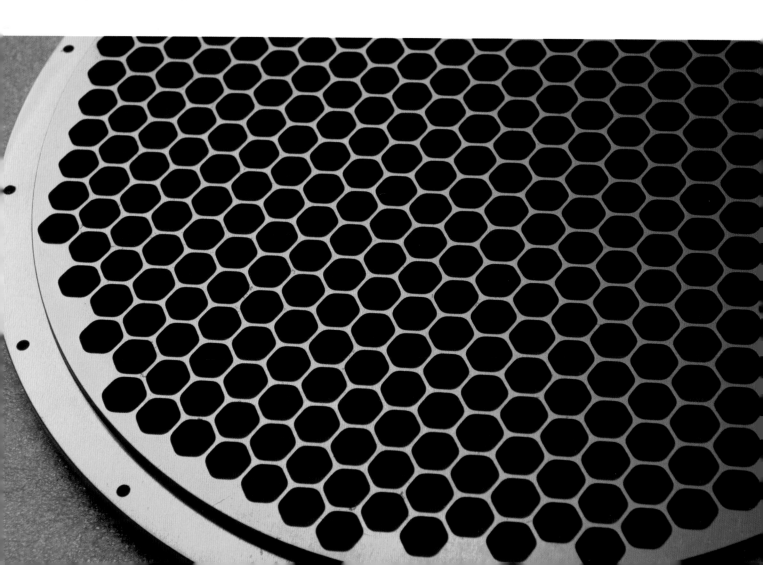

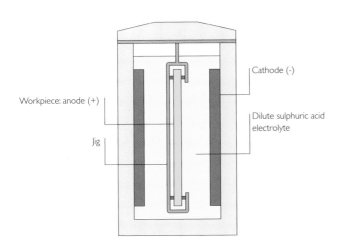

Workpiece: anode (+)

Jig

Cathode (-)

Dilute sulphuric acid electrolyte

VISUAL QUALITY	● ● ● ● ● ● ●
SPEED	● ● ● ● ● ● ●
TOOLING COST	● ● ● ● ● ● ●
UNIT COST	● ● ● ● ● ● ●
ENVIRONMENT	● ● ● ● ● ● ●

Related processes include: :
• Chromic Acid Anodizing
• Dip and Dye (Natural Anodizing)
• Hard Anodizing

Alternative and competing processes include:
• Electroplating
• Physical Vapour Deposition (PVD)
• Spray Painting
• Vacuum Metalizing

What is Aluminium Anodizing?

Aluminium anodizing takes place in an electrolytic solution, which is generally dilute sulphuric acid. A current is passed between the workpiece (anode) and electrode (cathode). This causes oxygen to gather on the surface of the part and it reacts with the base metal to form a porous oxide layer (aluminium produces aluminium oxide). The length of time in the bath, the temperature and the current determine the rate of film growth. It takes approximately 15 minutes to produce five microns (0.00019 in.) of anodic film.

QUALITY The process builds up the naturally occurring oxide layer on the surface of the metal. The film is light, hard, protective and self-healing; aluminium oxide is inert and among the hardest materials known to man.

TYPICAL APPLICATIONS Most aluminium in the automotive, consumer electronics and leisure industries is treated in this way.

COST AND SPEED There are no tooling costs, but jigs are required. Cycle time is between 30 minutes and six hours. Labour costs are minimal.

MATERIALS Aluminium, magnesium and titanium can be anodized. It is also possible to anodize zinc, niobium, hafnium and tantalum.

ENVIRONMENTAL IMPACTS Although acidic chemicals are used in the anodizing process there are no hazardous by-products. The baths are continuously filtered and recycled. Dissolved aluminium is filtered from the rinse tanks as aluminium hydroxide, which can be safely recycled or disposed of.

Satin red anodized aluminium (above) Anodizing can be applied to all types of finishes and textures, including satin, brushed, embossed and mirror polished. Only thin coatings will retain a high gloss finish and these are therefore not suitable for high-wear applications.

Jigs (above) Bespoke jigs formed to accommodate parts during the anodizing process. Parts have to be connected with a power source to be anodized. This can be done in two ways: they are either 'loose wired' or mounted onto a rigid jig. Jigs have a fixed point of contact which may be visible after anodizing. This is minimized by contacting the workpiece between two small points, or on an inconspicuous part of the product.

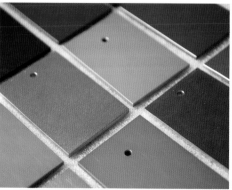

'Dip and dye' colour samples (left) The 'dip and dye' process can produce the widest range of colours, but it is the least UV stable and consistent, so is generally only used for decorative and indoor applications. Substantially more durable surface finishes and colour can be created on the surface of the base metal by depositing cobalt, or tin, metal salts in a process known as Anolok™. This is considerably more expensive and the colour range is limited.

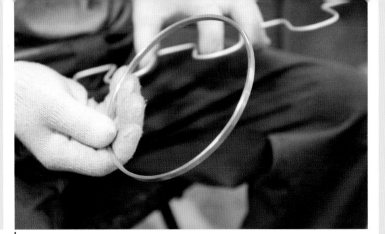

1

2

3

Case Study

'Dip and Dye' Anodizing Aluminium

Featured company Young Kwang
www.anodizing.or.kr

The metal rings are prepared and mounted onto an aluminium wire jig (image **1**). They will remain on the jig throughout the entire process.

Anodizing is made up of many stages including cleaning, anodizing, colouring and sealing. The processes takes place in a series of baths (image **2**) and can take up to six hours depending on the required finish. The anodized parts are dipped into a solution of gold dye (image **3**). The finish is sealed onto the surface of the aluminium in a bath of hot water with additives at a temperature of 98°C (208.4°F) (image **4**).

The anodic film is non-toxic and can be handled immediately after sealing. The finished parts are removed from the jig and inspected (image **5**).

4

5

Automated Spray Painting

The high gloss, high lustre and metallic finishes on many injection molded consumer goods, such as televisions, mobile phones and MP3 players, are produced by automated spray painting. Solvent- and water-based systems are both utilized although recently there has been a shift towards the latter for environmental reasons.

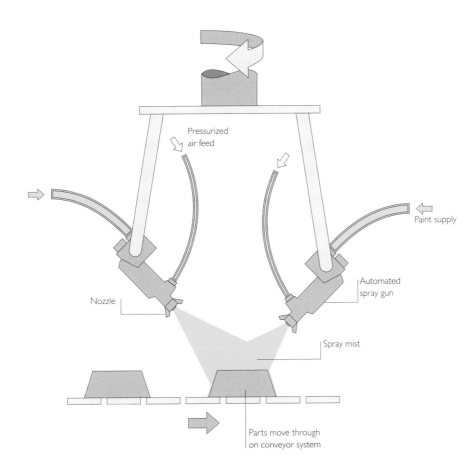

Pressurized
air feed

Paint supply

Nozzle

Automated
spray gun

Spray mist

Parts move through
on conveyor system

Essential Information

VISUAL QUALITY	◉◉◉◉◉◉◎◎
SPEED	◉◉◉◉◉◉◎◎
TOOLING COST	◉◉◉◉◉◉◎◎
UNIT COST	◉◉◉◉◉◎◎◎
ENVIRONMENT	◉◉◉◉◉◎◎◎

Alternative and competing processes include:
- Dip Molding
- Electroplating
- Flocking
- Metal Patination
- Polishing
- Vacuum Metalizing

What is Automated Spray Painting?

Automated systems are rapid and production is continuous. Either the products move through on a conveyor belt and pass underneath moving spray guns (pictured), or the products are stacked into a rotating jig and coated by computer-guided spray guns.

Spray guns use a jet of compressed air to atomize the paint into a fine mist. The atomized paint is blown out of the nozzle in an elliptical shape. The coating is applied onto the surface in an overlapping pattern. The speed of the conveyor, or rotating jig, is optimized with the speed of painting to maximize efficiency.

Conventional paints are made up of pigment, binder, thinner and additives. The role of the binder is to bond the pigment to the surface being coated. It determines the durability, finish, speed of drying and resistance to abrasion. These mixtures are dissolved or dispersed in either water or a solvent.

QUALITY Spray coatings are built up in thin layers, typically between five and 100 microns (0.0002–0.004 in.) thick. The level of sheen on the coating is categorized as matt (also known as egg shell), semi-gloss, satin (also known as silk) and gloss.

TYPICAL APPLICATIONS Spray painting is used in a vast range of applications including prototyping, low-volume and high-volume production.

COST AND SPEED There are no tooling costs, although jigs may be required. Cycle time is rapid for an automated process. Labour costs are minimal.

MATERIALS Almost all materials can be spray painted. Some surfaces have to be coated with an intermediate layer which is compatible with both the workpiece and the topcoat.

ENVIRONMENTAL IMPACTS Water-based paints are less toxic than solvent-borne. Spraying is usually carried out in a booth or cabinet to allow the paints to be recycled and disposed of safely.

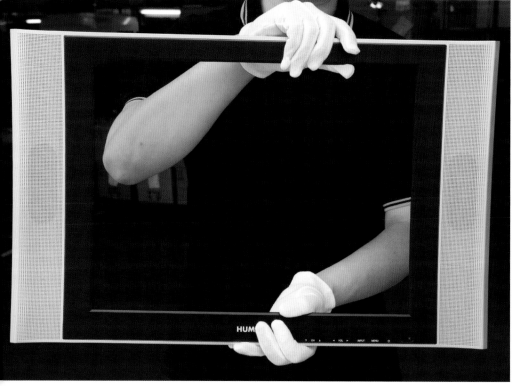

Spray-painted TV cover Entire surfaces can be painted, including different materials, to produce a seamless finish. Alternatively, a single material can be spray painted with masks to give the effect of contrasting materials. This TV cover is a single injection molding (page 40) that has been masked and sprayed gloss black and silver. The other way to achieve this is with multishot injection molding (page 44).

Case Study

Spray Painting an Injection Molded Part

Featured company Young Sung Tis Co. Ltd
www.youngsungtis.co.kr

Many mass-produced consumer goods are finished in this way. Spray painting is used to apply colour and provide surface protection. Injection molded parts are stacked in preparation for coating (image **1**).

This automated spray painting system consists of three spray guns which are mounted onto a spinning axis (image **2**). As the products move underneath the spray guns spin rapidly and so cover the surface of the parts with an even coating of paint (image **3**).

The parts move through an oven which reduces paint drying time and improves surface finish. Finally, the parts are carefully inspected under bright lamps and imperfect parts are removed and recycled (image **4**).

1

2   3

4

Electroplating

Electroplating is used to produce functional and decorative finishes. Thin layers of metal, from less than one micron (0.000039 in.) up to 25 microns (0.0098 in.) thick, are deposited on the surface of the workpiece in an electrochemical process. A strong metallurgical bond is formed between the base material and the coating.

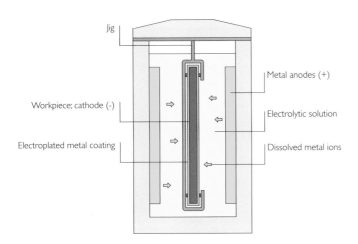

Jig

Workpiece; cathode (-)

Electroplated metal coating

Metal anodes (+)

Electrolytic solution

Dissolved metal ions

Essential Information

VISUAL QUALITY	●●●●●●●●
SPEED	●●●●●●●●
TOOLING COST	●●●●●●●●
UNIT COST	●●●●●●●●
ENVIRONMENT	●●●●●●●●

Alternative and competing processes include:

- Anodizing
- Electroforming
- Physical Vapour Deposition (PVD)
- Spray Painting
- Vacuum Metalizing

What is Electroplating?

Electroplating occurs in an electrolytic solution of the plating metal held in suspension in ionic form. When the workpiece is submerged and connected to a DC current a thin film of electroplating forms on its surface. The rate of deposition depends on the temperature and chemical content of the electrolyte.

As the thickness of electroplating builds up on the surface of the workpiece the ionic content of the electrolyte is replenished by dissolution of the metal anodes. The anodes are suspended in the electrolyte in a perforated container.

The thickness of electroplating depends on the application of the product and material. For example, nickel used as an intermediate levelling layer may be up to 10 microns (0.00039 in.), while electroplated gold needs to be only one micron (0.000039 in.) thick for decorative applications.

QUALITY Electroplated films are made up of pure metal or alloys. An integral layer is formed between the workpiece and metal coating because each metal ion forms a strong metallurgical bond with its neighbour.

TYPICAL APPLICATIONS Electroplated metal products include jewelry, trophies and tableware. Plastic examples include automotive trim, bathroom fittings, consumer electronics and cosmetic packaging.

COST AND SPEED There are no tooling costs, but jigs are required. Cycle time depends on the accuracy of the finish required and ranges from 30 minutes to several hours. Labour costs are minimal.

MATERIALS Most metals can be electroplated. The plastic that is most commonly electroplated is acrylonitrile butadiene styrene (ABS). It is able to withstand the 60°C (140°F) processing temperature, and it is possible to etch into the surface to form a relatively strong bond between it and the electroless plated metal.

ENVIRONMENTAL IMPACTS Many hazardous chemicals are used in all of the electroplating processes. They are carefully controlled with extraction and filtration to ensure minimal environmental impact.

Raw materials for electroplating Pure copper and nickel are two examples of the types of metals that are utilized as a coating material in the electroplating process. They are often used as intermediate layers and help to produce a very bright finish because they provide a certain amount of levelling. It is also possible to coat materials with a thin layer of tin, chrome, silver, gold and rhodium. These raw materials are placed into the electroplating bath along with the workpiece and are positively charged. Metal ions dissolve in the electrolytic solution and form the electroplated layer on the surface of the negatively charged workpiece.

1

2

Case Study

Gold Electroplating Jewelry

Featured company Daedo Inc. www.dae-do.co.kr

Mass production electroplating is a rapid process; the parts are moved through the cleaning and plating baths at high speed. Firstly, the cast zinc parts are coated with a thin layer of copper (image **1**). This intermediate layer provides a strong and compatible metallurgical bond between the zinc and next layer of metal electroplating, which is an alloy of zinc, lead and tin. Finally, a thin layer of gold is added electrochemically.

The parts are removed from the electroplating bath, centrifugally dried at high speed and stacked (image **2**). Each of the parts is carefully removed from the jig and placed on a tray in preparation for spraying (image **3**). A protective layer of polyurethane is sprayed onto the parts to prevent oxidization and discolouration (image **4**).

3

4

Vacuum Metalizing

The vacuum metalizing process is used to coat a wide range of materials to create the look of anodizing, chrome, gold and other metals. The finish ranges from half mirror to full mirror, depending on the coating thickness. Colour is added with topcoats.

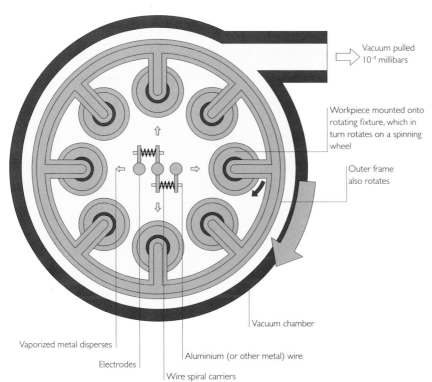

Vacuum pulled
10⁻⁴ millibars

Workpiece mounted onto
rotating fixture, which in
turn rotates on a spinning
wheel

Outer frame
also rotates

Vacuum chamber

Vaporized metal disperses

Electrodes

Wire spiral carriers

Aluminium (or other metal) wire

Essential Information

VISUAL QUALITY

SPEED

TOOLING COST

UNIT COST

ENVIRONMENT

Related processes include:
• Non-conductive Vacuum Metalizing

Alternative and competing processes include:
• Anodizing
• Electroplating
• Physical Vapour Deposition (PVD)
• Spray Painting

What is Vacuum Metalizing?

The workpieces are mounted onto rotating holding fixtures (custom made for each part), which are in turn rotated on spinning wheels. The assembly is suspended within a frame, which also rotates. All in all, the parts are being rotated around three parallel axes simultaneously. This is to ensure an even coating with line-of-sight geometry.

A vacuum is generated within the metalizing chamber. Then an electrical discharge is passed through the wire of aluminium (or other metal) by the electrodes. The combination of the electric current and high vacuum cause the almost pure metal to vaporize in an instant. It bursts into a plume of metal vapour which condenses on the relatively cool surface of the workpiece.

Notes for Designers

QUALITY Vacuum metalizing is used to increase the surface quality by improving reflectivity, wear and corrosion resistance. It also improves colouring capability.

TYPICAL APPLICATIONS Decorative uses include jewelry, sculptures, trophies, prototypes, kitchen utensils and ironmongery. Coatings can be functional, providing electromagnetic interference (EMI) or radio frequency (RF) shielding, improved wear resistance, heat deflection or light reflection (such as torch and automotive light reflectors). It is known as non-conductive vacuum metalling (NCVM) when applied as an ultra thin coating that does not affect radio signals. This is utilized to decorate injection molded plastic mobile phones.

COST AND SPEED There are no tooling costs. Cycle time is moderate (up to six hours). It is quite a labour intensive process; the parts have to be sprayed, loaded, unloaded and sprayed again.

MATERIALS Many materials are suitable, including metals, rigid and flexible plastics, resins, composites, ceramics and glass. Natural fibres are generally not suitable; it is very difficult to apply the vacuum if moisture is present.

ENVIRONMENTAL IMPACTS This process creates very little waste. Spraying the basecoat and topcoat has impacts equivalent to spray painting. Metalizing can be used to extend the life of products by increasing their resistance to corrosion and wear.

Vacuum metalized button set (above) It is possible to vacuum metalize complex and intricate shapes such as technical consumer electronic parts. These injection molded button sets have been vacuum metalized to look like bright gold.

Coloured vacuum metalizing (right) Vivid colours can be used to replicate anodized aluminium, bright chrome, silver, gold, copper or gunmetal, among others. The advantage of this is that relatively inexpensive materials can be formed and then vacuum metalized to give the look and feel of metal.

Vacuum Metalizing Brass Hinges

Featured company VMC Ltd www.vmclimited.co.uk

The workpieces, which are mounted onto their jigs, are sprayed with a basecoat and loaded onto the rotating holding fixtures (image 1).

The wire spiral holders that connect the positive and negative electrodes are loaded with aluminium wire (image 2) and the whole assembly is loaded into the vacuum chamber (image 3). Once a sufficient vacuum is reached, an electrical discharge is passed through the wire, causing the aluminium to vaporize (image 4).

The parts before and after they have been vacuum metalized appear markedly different (image 5).

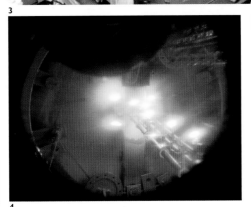

Glossary

CAD

Computer-aided design (CAD) is a general term used to cover computer programmes that assist with engineering and product design. Some of the most popular 3D packages include Professional Engineer, commonly known as Pro E, Rhino, SolidWorks, AutoCAD, Alias and Maya.

CAE

Computer-aided engineering is a general term used to cover the use of computer programmes in the design, simulation, analysis, production and optimization of products and assemblies. Examples include FEA and Moldflow (page 11).

CNC

Machining equipment that is operated by a computer is known as computer numerical control (CNC). The number of operational axes determines the types of geometries that can be achieved. Two axis, three axis and five axis are the most common (page 113).

Elastomer

A natural or synthetic material that exhibits elastic properties: the ability to deform under load and return to its original shape once the load is removed.

FEA

Finite element analysis is a computer-simulation technique that uses a numerical system that assists with engineering calculations by dividing an object into smaller parts, known as finite elements, to analyse designs, improve molding efficiency and predict part performance post-molding.

Ferrous

Metals that contain iron such as steel. See also non-ferrous.

Flash

Excess material that is formed in the small gaps between the different parts of a mold during the molding process.

FRP

Molded plastic reinforced with lengths of fibre – including carbon, aramid, glass or natural material such as cotton, hemp or jute – is known as fibre-reinforced plastic (FRP). They are formed by a range of processes including DMC and SMC molding (see compression molding, page 14) and injection molding (page 38). See also GRP.

GRP

Molded plastic reinforced with lengths of glass fibre. Injection molded (page 38) glass fibre-reinforced plastic (GRP) has a very short fibre length (up to 3 mm, 0.118 in.), whereas DMC and SMC molded (page 20) plastic has long or continuous lengths of glass fibre reinforcement. See also FRP.

Hardwood

Wood from deciduous and broad-leaved trees such as birch, beech, ash and oak.

Mold

A hollow form, which is used to shape materials in their liquid or plastic state, or a concave or convex 3D profile over which materials are formed in their solid state.

Monomer

A small, simple compound that can be joined with other similar compounds to form long chains known as polymers.

Non-ferrous

Metals that do not contain iron such as aluminium alloys and copper alloys. See also ferrous.

Pattern

An original design or prototype that is reproduced to form a mold, such as in investment casting (page 66). This mold can then be used to produce many identical parts.

Polymer

A natural or synthetic compound made up of long chains of repeating identical monomers.

RAL

Reichsausschuss für Lieferbedingungen is a German colour chart system used mainly in paint and pigment colour specification.

Resin

A natural or synthetic semi-solid or solid substance, produced by polymerization or extraction from plants, and used in plastics, varnishes and paints.

Shore hardness

The hardness of a plastic, rubber or elastomer is measured by the depth of indentation of a shaped metal foot on a measuring instrument known as a durometer. The depth of indentation is measured on a scale of 0 to 100; higher numbers indicate harder materials. These tests are generally used to indicate the flexibility of a material. The two most popular are Shore A and Shore D. There is not a strong correlation between different scales.

Softwood

Wood from coniferous and typical evergreen trees such as pine, spruce, fir and cedar.

Thermoplastic

A polymeric material that becomes soft and pliable when heated. It can be shaped and re-shaped by a range of molding processes such as injection molding (page 38).

Thermosetting plastic

A material formed by heating, catalyzing, or mixing two parts to trigger a one-way polymeric reaction. Unlike most thermoplastics, thermosetting plastics form cross links between the polymer chains, which cannot be undone and so this material cannot be re-shaped or re-molded once cured. Thermosetting plastics tend to have a superior resistance to fatigue and chemical attack compared with thermoplastics.

Tool

Another term for mold.

VDI

Surface texture is measured on the Association of German Engineers' VDI scale. The VDI scale is comparable with roughness average (Ra) 0.32–18 microns (0.000013–0.00071 in.).

Featured Companies

Ajin Tech
420 Eun-san ri, Jin we meun
Pyung-thck ci
Kyung kin do
South Korea
www.apchul.com

Alessi SpA
Via Privata Alessi, 6
28887 Crusinallo Di
Omegna – VB
Italy
www.alessi.com

Bang & Olufsen
Peter Bangs Vej 15
7600 Struer
Denmark
www.bang-olufsen.com

Biomega
Skoubogade 1, 1. MF
1158 Copenhagen
Denmark
www.biomega.dk

Boss Design
Boss Drive
Dudley
West Midlands DY2 8SZ
United Kingdom
www.boss-design.co.uk

Branson Ultrasonics Corporation
158 Edinburgh Avenue
Slough Trading Estate
Slough
Berkshire SL1 4UE
United Kingdom
www.bransonultrasonics.com

Branson (UK)
686 Stirling Road
Slough Trading Estate
Slough
Berkshire SL1 4ST
United Kingdom
www.branson-plasticsjoin.com

Cove Industries
Industries House
18 Invincible Road
Farnborough
Hampshire GU14 7QU
United Kingdom
www.cove-industries.co.uk

Cromwell Plastics
53–54 New Street, Quarry Bank
Dudley
West Midlands DY5 2AZ
United Kingdom
www.cromwellplastics.co.uk

Daedo Inc.
13–18 Sungsu 2 Dong
Sungdong-Gu
Seoul
South Korea
www.dae-do.co.kr

Elmill Group
139A Engineer Road
West Wilts Trading Estate
Wiltshire BA13 4JW
United Kingdom
www.elmill.com

ENL Limited
Units 6–8, Victoria Trading Estate
Kiln Road
Portsmouth
Hampshire PO3 5LP
United Kingdom
www.enl.co.uk

Ercol Furniture Ltd
Summerleys Road
Princes Risborough
Buckinghamshire HP27 9PX
United Kingdom
www.ercol.com

Hartley Greens & Co.
(Leeds Pottery)
Anchor Road
Longton
Stoke-on-Trent ST3 5ER
United kingdom
www.hartleygreens.com

HTC
23 Xinghua Road
Taoyuan 330
Taiwan, R. O. C.
www.htc.com

Interfoam Limited
15–17 Ronald Close
Woburn Road Industrial Estate
Kempston
Bedford MK42 7SH
www.interfoam.co.uk

Kaysersberg Plastics
Madleaze Industrial Estate
Bristol Road
Gloucester GL1 5SG
United Kingdom
www.kayplast.com

Kaysersberg Plastics (France)
BP No. 27
68240 Kaysersberg
France
www.kayplast.com

Lloyd Loom of Spalding
Wardentree Lane
Pinchbeck
Spalding
Lincolnshire PE11 3SY
United Kingdom
www.lloydloom.com

Luceplan SpA
Via E.T. Moneta 46
20161 Milan
Italy
www.luceplan.com

Magis SpA
Via Magnadola, 15
31045 Motta di Livenza (TV)
Italy
www.magisdesign.com

Mathmos
22–24 Old Street
London EC1V 9AP
United Kingdom
www.mathmos.co.uk

Metal Injection Mouldings Ltd
Davenport Lane
Altringham
Cheshire WA14 5DS
United Kingdom
www.metalinjection.co.uk

MiMtec Limited
Unit D, Jten Trade Park
Wickham Road
Fareham
Hampshire PO16 7JB
United Kingdom
www.mimtec.co.uk

Moldflow Corporation
492 Old Connecticut Path
Suite 401
Framingham, MA 01701
USA
www.moldflow.com

PI Castings
Davenport Lane
Altringham
Cheshire WA14 5DS
United Kingdom
www.pi-castings.co.uk

Pipecraft
Units 6–7, Wayside
Commerce Way
Lancing
West Sussex BN15 8SW
United Kingdom
www.pipecraft.co.uk

ProCut Ltd
Unit 3, Towerfield Close
Shoeburyness
Essex SS3 9AP
United Kingdom
www.procutuk.co.uk

Product Partners Design
The Old Warehouse
Church Street
Biggleswade
Bedfordshire SG18 0JS
United Kingdom
www.productpartners.co.uk

Rega Research
No. 6, Coopers Way
Temple Farm Industrial Estate
Southend-on-Sea
Essex SS2 5TE
www.rega.co.uk

Rexite SpA
Via Edison 7
20090 Cusago
Milan
Italy
www.rexite.it

RubberTech2000
Whimsey Trading Estate
Cinderford
Gloucestershire GL14 3JA
United Kingdom
www.rubbertech2000.co.uk

Smile Plastics
Mansion House
Ford
Shrewsbury SY5 9LZ
United Kingdom
www.smile-plastics.co.uk

Superform Aluminium
Cosgrove Close
Worcester WR3 8UA
United Kingdom
www.superform-aluminium.com

Superform USA
6825 Jurupa Avenue
Riverside, CA 92517–5375
USA
www.superformusa.com

Taekwang Techno Co. Ltd
(31B–1L) Namdong Industrial
Complex
#608 Namchon-Dong
Namdong-Gu, Incheon
South Korea
www.tkmold.co.kr

Thonet GmbH
Michael-Thonet-Straße 1
35066 Frankenberg
Germany
www.thonet.de

VMC Ltd
Trafalgar Works
Station Road
Chertsey KT16 8BR
United Kingdom
www.vmclimited.co.uk

Young Kwang
125–1, Ne don
Oh jung gu, Buchun ci
Kyung ki do
South Korea
www.anodizing.or.kr

Young Sung Tis Co. Ltd
510–3BA, Siwha
Jung-wang dong,
Ci hung ci, Kyung ki do
South Korea
www.youngsungtis.co.kr

Further Reading

Alessi, Alberto, *The Dream Factory: Alessi Since 1921* (Milan: Electa/Alessi, 1998)

Ashby, Mike, and Kara Johnson, *Materials and Design: The Art and Science of Material Selection in Product Design* (Oxford and Boston: Butterworth-Heinemann, 2002)

Beylerian, George M., Andrew Dent and Anita Moryadas (eds), *Material ConneXion: The Global Resource of New and Innovative Materials for Architects, Artists, and Designers* (London: Thames & Hudson and Hoboken, NJ: J. Wiley, 2005)

Brownell, Blaine (ed.), *Transmaterial: A Catalog of Materials that Redefine Our Physical Environment* (New York: Princeton Architectural Press, 2006)

Byars, Mel, *50 Chairs: Innovations in Design and Materials* (Crans-Près-Céligny: RotoVision and New York: Watson-Guptill Publishers, 1996)

Byars, Mel, *50 Lights: Innovations in Design and Materials* (Crans-Près-Céligny: RotoVision, 1997)

Byars, Mel, *50 Products: Innovations in Design and Materials* (Crans-Près-Céligny: RotoVision, 1998)

Byars, Mel, *50 Tables: Innovations in Design and Materials* (Crans-Près-Céligny: RotoVision, 1998)

Guidot, Raymond (ed.), *Industrial Design: Techniques and Materials* (Paris: Flammarion, 2006)

Harper, Charles A., *Handbook of Materials for Product Design*, 3rd edn (Columbus: McGraw-Hill, 2001)

Hudson, Jennifer, *Process: 50 Product Designs from Concept to Manufacture* (London: Laurence King, 2008)

IDSA (Industrial Designers Society of America), *Design Secrets. Products: 50 Real-Life Projects Uncovered* (Massachusetts: Rockport Publishers, 2003)

IDTC (International Design Trend Centre), *How Things Are Made: Manufacturing Guide for Designers* (Seoul: Agbook, 2003)

Kula, Daniel, Elodie Turnaux and Quentin Hirsinger, *Materiology: The Creative Industry's Guide to Materials and Technologies* (Boston, Mass.: Birkhäuser, 2008)

Lefteri, Chris, *Making It: Manufacturing Techniques for Product Design* (London: Laurence King, 2007)

Lefteri, Chris, *Materials for Inspirational Design* (Mies: RotoVision, 2006)

Lesko, Jim, *Industrial Design: Materials and Manufacturing Guide* (Hoboken, NJ: J. Wiley, 1999)

Manzini, Ezio, *The Material of Invention: Materials and Design* (Milan: Arcadia, 1986 and Cambridge, Mass.: MIT Press, 1989)

Mori, Toshiko (ed.), *Immaterial/ Ultramaterial: Architecture, Design, and Materials* (Cambridge, Mass.: Harvard Design School in association with George Braziller, 2002)

Saville, Laurel, and Brooke Stoddard, *Design Secrets. Furniture: 50 Real-Life Projects Uncovered* (Massachusetts: Rockport Publishers, 2008)

Stattmann, Nicola, *Ultra Light Super Strong: A New Generation of Design Materials* (Basel and Boston: Birkhäuser, 2003)

van Onna, Edwin, *Material World: Innovative Structures and Finishes for Interiors* (Amsterdam/Basel and Boston: Frame Publishers/Birkhäuser, 2003)

Illustration Credits

Rob Thompson photographed the processes, materials and products in this book. The author would like to acknowledge the following for permission to reproduce photographs and CAD visuals.

Introduction
Page 8 (Pedalite exploded): Product Partners
Page 9 (Bang & Olufsen speakers): Bang & Olufsen
Page 10 (Thonet 214): Thonet
Page 10 (HTC Legend): HTC
Page 11 (Moldflow analysis): Moldflow

Injection Molding
Page 42 (Magis Air-Chair): Magis
Page 45 (images 1, 2 and 3): Taekwang Techno
Page 46 (Luceplan Lightdisc): Luceplan

Metal Injection Molding
Pages 50–51 (all images): Metal Injection Mouldings

Foam Molding
Page 54 (image 1): Boss Design
Page 57 (Sona Chair): Boss Design

High Pressure Die Casting
Page 64 (Virtual analysis of Chair One): Magis
Page 65 (image 1): Magis

Investment Casting
Pages 68–69 (all images): PI Castings

Metal Press Forming
Page 72 (Alessi Mediterraneo Bowl): Alessi
Page 73 (image 1): Alessi
Page 75 (image 1): Rexite

Metal Spinning
Page 83 (image 1): Mathmos

Tube and Section Bending
Page 86 (image 1): Thonet
Page 87 (Thonet S 5000): Thonet
Page 88 (Thonet S 826): Thonet

Superplastic Forming
Page 96 (title image): Superform Aluminium
Page 98 (Biomega MN01 bike): Biomega
Page 98 (Superplastic aluminium samples): Superform Aluminium
Page 99 (all images): Superform Aluminium

Steam Bending
Page 110 (image 1): Thonet
Page 111 (Thonet A 660 Loop Chair): Thonet

Acknowledgments

The technical detail and accuracy of the book's content is the result of the extraordinary generosity of many individuals and organizations. Their knowledge of processes and materials and their years of hands-on experience were fundamental in putting this book together. Thank you to all of the companies that have been featured. Their contact details are given on pages 187 to 189.

I would like to thank the book's designer Chris Perkins, the editor Ilona de Nemethy Sanigar and Thames & Hudson for their continued support and dedication to producing the highest standard of work.

The support, encouragement and input from colleagues, family and friends has been invaluable throughout. I would particularly like to thank Young-Yun Kim, who worked very hard to make sure we got some excellent case studies in South Korea.

This book is dedicated to Mum, Dad, Ansel, Murray and Lina.

Index

Page numbers in **bold** refer to references in the 'What is' and Case Study texts; page numbers in *italics* refer to references in the Essential Information and caption texts